MW00856910

THE IDEA OF TRADITION
IN THE LATE MODERN WORLD

THE IDEA OF TRADITION
IN THE LATE MODERN WORLD

An Ecumenical and Interreligious Conversation

∽

Thomas Albert Howard

CASCADE *Books* · Eugene, Oregon

THE IDEA OF TRADITION IN THE LATE MODERN WORLD
An Ecumenical and Interreligious Conversation

Copyright © 2020 Thomas Albert Howard. All rights reserved. Except for brief quotations in critical publications or reviews, no part of this book may be reproduced in any manner without prior written permission from the publisher. Write: Permissions, Wipf and Stock Publishers, 199 W. 8th Ave., Suite 3, Eugene, OR 97401.

Cascade Books
An Imprint of Wipf and Stock Publishers
199 W. 8th Ave., Suite 3
Eugene, OR 97401

www.wipfandstock.com

PAPERBACK ISBN: 978-1-5326-7889-9
HARDCOVER ISBN: 978-1-5326-7890-5
EBOOK ISBN: 978-1-5326-7891-2

Cataloguing-in-Publication data:

Names: Howard, Thomas Albert, editor.

Title: The idea of tradition in the late modern world : an ecumenical and interreligious conversation / edited by Thomas Albert Howard.

Description: Eugene, OR: Cascade Books, 2020 | Includes bibliographical references and index.

Identifiers: ISBN 978-1-5326-7889-9 (paperback) | ISBN 978-1-5326-7890-5 (hardcover) | ISBN 978-1-5326-7891-2 (ebook)

Subjects: LCSH: Tradition (Religion). | Tradition (Philosophy).

Classification: AZ103 .I33 2020 (print) | AZ103 (ebook)

Manufactured in the U.S.A.   JANUARY 17, 2020

To the faculty, staff, and students of Christ College
at Valparaiso University

Table of Contents

Acknowledgments

I AM GRATEFUL FOR the help, support, and encouragement of the following people: Peter Kanelos, Jennifer Prough, Susan Van Zanten, Mel Piehl, Mark Schwehn, Patrice Weil, Sharon Dybel, Slavica Jakelic, Matthew Puffer, Claire Ehr, Ethan Stoppenhagen, Agnes R. Howard, Ronald Rittgers, Mark Biermann, Mark Heckler, Nicholas Denysenko, Joseph Goss, Joseph Creech, Kevin Gary, Noelle Canty, and Linda Schmidt. The book is dedicated to the faculty, staff, and students, past and present, of Christ College at Valparaiso University. May the College continue to strive to send students into the world characterized by a *sapiens et eloquens pietas*.

Contributors

DAVID BENTLEY HART
Fellow of the Institute of Advanced Studies at the University of Notre Dame
David Bentley Hart is an American Orthodox Christian philosophical theologian, cultural commentator, and polemicist. He has taught at the University of Virginia, the University of St. Thomas (Minnesota), Duke Divinity School, and Loyola College in Maryland. During the 2014–2015 academic year, Hart was Danforth Chair at Saint Louis University in the theological studies department. In 2015, Hart was appointed as Templeton Fellow at the University of Notre Dame Institute for Advanced Study. He is author or editor of eleven books, including *The Beauty of the Infinite: The Aesthetics of Christian Truth* (Eerdmans, 2003); *Atheist Delusions: The Christian Revolution and Its Fashionable Enemies* (Yale University Press, 2009); *The Experience of God: Being, Consciousness, Bliss* (Yale University Press, 2013); *The Hidden and the Manifest: Essays in Theology and Metaphysics* (Eerdmans, 2017); and *The New Testament: A Translation* (Yale University Press, 2017). Hart's book *Atheist Delusions* was awarded the Michael Ramsey Prize in Theology in 2011.

JAMES L. HEFT, SM.
Director of the Institute for Advanced Catholic Studies at the University of Southern California; Alton M. Brooks Professor of Religion at the University of Southern California
Father James L. Heft, SM, is a priest in the Society of Mary and a leader for more than twenty years in Catholic higher education. He spent many years at the University of Dayton, serving as chair of the theology department for six years, provost of the University for eight years, and chancellor for ten years. He left the University of Dayton in 2006 to found the Institute

for Advanced Catholic Studies at the University of Southern California in Los Angeles, where he now serves as the Alton Brooks Professor of Religion and president of the Institute. He has written and edited 13 books and published more than 175 articles and book chapters. Most recently, he edited *Learned Ignorance: Intellectual Humility Among Jews, Christians, and Muslims* (Oxford University Press, 2011); *Catholicism and Interreligious Dialogue* (Oxford University Press, 2011); and *In the Lógos of Love: Promise and Predicament in Catholic Intellectual Life* (Oxford University Press, 2015). His book, *Catholic High Schools: Facing the New Realities* (Oxford University Press, 2011), was listed as a "bestseller" in a recent Oxford University Press catalogue. In 2011, the Association of Catholic Colleges and Universities presented him with the Theodore M. Hesburgh Award for his long and distinguished service to Catholic higher education. He is currently working on a book, *Catholic Higher Education: Its Condition and Future.*

THOMAS ALBERT HOWARD
Professor of Humanities and History and holder of the Duesenberg Chair in Christian Ethics, Valparaiso University
Professor Howard is affiliated with Christ College, Valparaiso's humanities-based honors college. He also serves as Senior Fellow for the Lilly Fellows Program in Humanities and the Arts. Prior to coming to Valparaiso, he taught at Gordon College, where he founded and directed the Jerusalem and Athens Forum honors program and led the Center for Faith and Inquiry. He is the author or editor of many books, including *The Pope and the Professor: Pius IX, Ignaz von Döllinger, and the Quandary of the Modern Age* (Oxford University Press, 2017); *Remembering the Reformation: An Inquiry into the Meanings of Protestantism* (Oxford University Press, 2016); and *Protestantism after 500 Years* (Oxford University Press, 2016), edited with Mark A. Noll. His writings have appeared in peer-reviewed journals, such as the *Journal of the History of Ideas*; the *Journal of the American Academy of Religion*; and in more general venues, such as *Hedgehog Review; Wall Street Journal; National Interest; Christian Century; First Things*; and *Commonweal*. His next book, *The Faiths of Others: Modern History and the Rise of Interreligious Dialogue,* will be published by Yale University Press.

EBRAHIM MOOSA
Professor of Islamic Studies at the University of Notre Dame

Ebrahim Moosa is professor of Islamic Studies at the University of Notre Dame in the Keough School of Global Affairs, with appointments in the history department and the Kroc Institute for International Peace Studies. Professor Moosa held previous appointments at Duke University, Stanford University, and the University of Cape Town. He is an expert in Islamic thought, covering modern and premodern Islamic law, theology, contemporary Muslim ethics, and political thought. His *What is a Madrasa?*, (University of North Carolina Press, 2015), is an important study on South Asia's traditional Islamic seminaries. He has also published widely in medieval Islamic thought, with special reference to the major twelfth-century Muslim thinker, Abu Hamid al-Ghazali (d. 1111). His prize-winning book, *Ghazali and the Poetics of Imagination* (University of North Carolina Press, 2005), was awarded the Best First Book in the History of Religions by the American Academy of Religion. His other publications include several co-edited books.

DAVID NOVAK
Richard and Dorothy Shiff Chair of Jewish Studies, University of Toronto
Rabbi David Novak holds the J. Richard and Dorothy Shiff Chair of Jewish Studies as professor of religion and philosophy at the University of Toronto, where he is a member of University College and the Joint Centre for Bioethics. He is a fellow of the Royal Society of Canada (FRSC), a fellow of the American Academy for Jewish Research, and a founder, vice president, and coordinator of the Panel of Inquiry on Jewish Law of the Union for Traditional Judaism. From 1989–1996, he was the Edgar M. Bronfman Professor of Modern Judaic Studies at the University of Virginia, and he has previously taught at Oklahoma City University, Old Dominion University, the Jewish Theological Seminary of America, and Baruch College of the City University of New York. Novak is the author of sixteen books, the last two being *Tradition in the Public Sphere: A David Novak Reader*, edited by Randi Rashkover and Martin Kavka (Eerdmans, 2008), and *In Defense of Religious Liberty* (ISI Books, 2009). His book *Covenantal Rights* (Princeton University Press, 2000) won the American Academy of Religion Award for "best book in constructive religious thought" in 2000. Novak is the subject of Matthew Levering's book, *Jewish-Christian Dialogue and the Life of Wisdom: Engagements with the Theology of David Novak* (Continuum, 2010).

SARAH HINLICKY WILSON

Editor of "Lutheran Forum"; Former Visiting Professor at the Institute for Ecumenical Research, Strasbourg, France

Rev. Dr. Sarah Hinlicky Wilson has been the editor of the theological quarterly *Lutheran Forum* for more than a decade. Since 2008, she has worked with the Institute for Ecumenical Research in Strasbourg, France, first as an assistant research professor and as a visiting professor since 2016. She has published two books in her areas of ecumenical expertise, *Woman, Women, and the Priesthood in the Trinitarian Theology of Elisabeth Behr-Sigel* (T&T Clark, 2015) and *A Guide to Pentecostal Movements for Lutherans* (Wipf and Stock, 2016). She has also written a book available in Chinese translation only, *An Influence Beyond 500 Years: Martin Luther Still Speaks Today*. Additionally, she has published more than a hundred articles on theological topics in venues both scholarly and popular. Rev. Wilson has spoken and taught widely on topics dealing with Lutheran and ecumenical theology across the US and around the world. In 2010, she and her husband, Andrew L. Wilson, retraced Luther's footsteps from Germany to Rome on the 500th anniversary of the reformer's famous pilgrimage, blogging about the experience at hereiwalk.org. Rev. Wilson now lives with her husband and son in Tokyo, where they work as missionaries with the Japan Evangelical Lutheran Church.

Introduction

Thomas Albert Howard
Valparaiso University

WE LIVE IN AN "age of accelerations," according to the *New York Times* columnist Thomas Friedman—an era in which technology, cultural norms, the workplace, social institutions, family structures, and much more appear to be changing with increasing rapidity.[1] In a similar vein, the late Polish sociologist Zygmunt Bauman once described our cultural moment as "liquid modernity"—his shorthand for the disorienting sense of flux and fluidity that many feel in the face of forces such as globalization, pluralism, specialization, urbanization, technological change, and more.[2] If these analyses are true, or even partly true, several questions present themselves to communities of faith: how can a religious tradition be faithfully observed, insightfully thought about, and successfully transmitted to succeeding generations in such a cultural climate? At a more general level, what exactly is "tradition" and how might a better understanding of it contribute to human flourishing in our present-day milieu?[3] Finally, what role do/should academic institutions and scholars play in passing down a (religious) tradition while keeping it engaged with but not wholly determined by present-day realities?

---

1. Friedman, *Thank You for Being Late*.

2. Bauman, *Liquid Modernity*. See also Heaphy, *Late Modernity and Social Change*.

3. On contemporary pluralism and religion in general, see Eck, *New Religious America*; Berger, *Many Altars of Modernity*.

These are the principal questions that inform this book. But the book also owes its origins to a specific occasion: a conference marking the fiftieth anniversary of Christ College, Valparaiso University's humanities-based honors college. Founded in 1966–67 by then University President O. P. Kretzmann (1901–1975), Christ College is among the oldest honors colleges in the United States. As an interdisciplinary liberal arts institution in the Lutheran tradition, as its website states, "Christ College is dedicated to the cultivation of intellectual, moral, and spiritual virtues. The College's name suggests its compatibility with Valparaiso University's definition of itself as a university in the *Christian intellectual tradition*."[4]

Commemorative occasions concentrate the mind; they help us remember where we have come from and where we are going—or ought to be going. They jolt us from the tyranny of the urgent and the complacency of the present to ruminate on longer stretches of time and deeper senses of purpose. The leadership and faculty of Christ College felt this jolt as we prepared for and marked our "golden" anniversary. A visit to the university's archives helped me—a relative newcomer to the faculty—grasp the original goals of the College and, by extension, what direction our commemorative conference ought to take. Three items in particular struck me.

First, although born under specifically Lutheran auspices, the College aimed from its inception to be outward-looking and ecumenical in religious identity. In an early blueprint for the College from 1964, President Kretzmann stressed that the College should "transcend denominational lines," welcoming students from a variety of backgrounds with different points of view. It was not to be Luther College or Wittenberg or Wartburg, but *Christ* College. As such, the College has enrolled students from many Christian denominations as well as from other faith traditions and even no faith traditions. At the same time, the College did not and does not fancy itself as having come from nowhere; it is rooted in a particular tradition, albeit one that, in its better moments, has striven for a broad-minded Christian catholicity and critical engagement with the churning pluralism of the contemporary world. Finally, its founding impulses suggested that Christ College should bring the world of faith and the world of intellect—Tertullian's "Jerusalem" and "Athens"—into creative, fruitful conversation, recognizing that modernity and its malcontents regrettably have too often banished the two into separate, non-interacting domains. The College was established to work against this tendency, as the founding blueprint holds:

4. Valparaiso University, "History" (emphasis added).

2

In all areas of the work of the college there should be a fusion of high intelligence and high religion. This means that in both areas the full implications of the Christian indicatives and imperatives should be worked out in daily life and [in the] work of the student. It is in this particular emphasis that Christ College ought to make its greatest and most singular contribution. Face to face with the explosion in human knowledge [i.e., academic specialization] this emphasis should lead to an appreciation of the cosmic and universal nature of the Christian Gospel.[5]

One could hardly find a better description of what we sought from our conference: "A fusion of high intelligence and high religion," a bracing, Johannine appreciation of the cosmic implications of the gospel or what the second-century theologian Justin Martyr called the *logos spermatikos*, the life-giving, reason-embracing, intellectually-hospitable seminal Word of God.[6] We desired a roster of scholars with unimpeachable academic credentials, but we also sought those who spoke *from*, and not merely *about*, their respective religious traditions, whose habits of mind and heart had been formed within a particular tradition. Additionally, we desired ecumenical and interreligious breadth—hence a line-up reflecting Eastern Orthodox, Catholic, Protestant, Jewish, and Muslim points of view, with the scholars bringing insights and perspectives drawn from their respective traditions to the table.

And, alas, this brings us back to the thorny question of tradition. It is commonplace in conversations about tradition to make a distinction made famous by the late church historian Jaroslav Pelikan (once on the faculty at Christ College). "Tradition," Pelikan wrote in his *Vindication of Tradition*, "is the living faith of the dead, traditionalism is the dead faith of the living. . . . [But] traditionalism . . . gives tradition a bad name."[7] By *tradition*, many people indeed mean *traditionalism*, which, in Pelikan's lexicon, denotes something more like *preservation*, a fussy, highly protective handing down of something from one generation to the next without the slightest addition or modification. Reflective theorists of the concept of tradition, however, tell us that this spectacularly misses the mark, for truly living, vibrant traditions *are* capable of change, adaptation, and development. Yet such

5. This document has been posted online. See Kretzmann, "Blueprint for Christ College"; "Destiny of a Christian University."

6. Dupuis, "Cosmic Christ in the Early Fathers"; Ndoumai, "Justin Martyr." See also Chadwick, *Early Christian Thought*, 9–22.

7. Pelikan, *Vindication of Tradition*, 65.

traditions do not welcome change of just any sort but rather judiciously distinguish which ones to embrace and which to eschew, which ones fit and which ones do not, which adaptations are helpful and which might distort. For this reason, David Bentley Hart tells us in his chapter that the idea of tradition is "incorrigibly equivocal. . . . It entails a certain necessary ambiguity regarding what kind of continuity it is meant to describe: in one sense, what is at issue is the continuity of unalterable practices and immutable beliefs." In another sense, however, Hart recognizes that tradition is always a "dynamic process, one that accommodates ceaseless alteration without taking leave of the original impulse or truth that this process supposedly enucleates over time." Both senses are indispensable, he concludes, and "any tradition that cannot be justified in both ways at once, at any given moment, is almost certainly one that is moribund."[8]

Tradition should be distinguished from two other, related concepts: *history* and *memory*. One of modernity's intellectual hallmarks has been the development of historical modes of inquiry and criticism—what scholars sometimes call historicism.[9] Pioneered in the nineteenth century, especially in German-speaking lands, by figures such as Leopold von Ranke and Ferdinand Christian Baur, historicism, applied to sacred texts, revolutionized biblical criticism and church history during this time. Critical historical inquiry has in fact posed a threat to tradition insofar as it sometimes removes the nimbus of timelessness and authority from hallowed individuals and events.[10] Ernst Troeltsch famously called this the "crisis of historicism" and regarded it as one of the greatest ruptures in Western thought.[11] Nevertheless, more attentive historical inquiry has prodded religious traditions to excise unwarranted accretions and spurious claims to distinguish more insightfully between the essential and the non-essential, the authentic and the counterfeit. Determining exactly what rightly belongs to a tradition and what might be expurgated or demoted in significance, however, often results in contentious processes, sometimes pitting scholars against ecclesiastical leaders, *homo academicus* against seats of religious authority. In what follows, this is clearly seen in James L. Heft's discussion of the Catholic

8. See chapter 3.

9. See Iggers, "Historicism."

10. Howard, *Religion and the Rise of Historicism*, 78–109. Admittedly, nineteenth-century historicism has earlier roots. See Morrow, "Acid of History"; Legaspi, *Death of Scripture*.

11. Troeltsch, "Die Krisis des Historismus."

Church during the Modernist crisis of the early twentieth century and during the Second Vatican Council in the 1960s. Something similar is afoot today in the Muslim world, as Ebrahim Moosa argues in chapter 4.[12]

Tradition should also not be confused with memory—and the related notions of collective or institutional memory—even though the two are closely related. Memory implies a more direct experience of something that is then remembered at a later time. Memory, however, means not only recollecting something but also adding nothing. It seeks accuracy, not continuity, even if achieving the right type of continuity might well be predicated on accurate memory. Still, memory stands closer to preservation. But tradition is open to addition, to change, and to renewal if what is added comports well with and furthers the goals of the tradition—perhaps even in an unprecedented imaginative fashion—even while demonstrating a certain indispensable continuity with the past. Determining exactly what can be added—not to mention when, why, and how—are, again, often messy, protracted processes involving various constituents of a tradition as well as the living in conversation with the dead. These processes constitute, in Alasdair MacIntyre's pithy definition of tradition, "an argument extended over time."[13]

Such an ongoing argument is perhaps an "unending task," according to the philosopher Josef Pieper; and for religious traditions, this is exactly what theology means: "The translation, which has to be revised over and over again under continually changing circumstances, of the 'original texts' of the *tradita* into a form which can be understood by the present historical moment."[14] Similarly, Yves Congar, the great Dominican theologian of Vatican II, once recognized that while tradition, literally understood, is something that is "received," "passed down" from the past, "it is also present-day ... ever fresh and alive; using its inherited riches, it answers the unexpected questions of today," preserving in the process certain essential elements while becoming something different than what it was before the new questions arose.[15] In this sense, tradition is "ever ancient, ever new," to borrow words from Augustine.[16] The oak becomes a tree not by simply negating

---

12. On the construction of the phrase "Muslim world," see Aynde, *Idea of the Muslim World*.

13. MacIntyre, *Whose Justice?*, 12.

14. Pieper, *Tradition*, 45.

15. Congar, *Meaning of Tradition*, 157.

16. Augustine, *Confessions*, 231.

the acorn but rather by faithfully realizing all of its latent possibilities over a period of time.

What characterizes our "present historical moment," to use the language of Pieper, and how does its many facets impinge upon religious traditions? This is not the place to review the sprawling literature on terms such as *modernity, postmodernism, postmodernity, late modernity*, and the like.[17] I have settled on "late modernity" because I am persuaded that more continuities exist between what we usually mean by modernity—dated usually to the eighteenth-century Enlightenment and the global rise of Western power and commercial capitalism—and our own present-day milieu. While not without merit, *post*modern suggests a more radical break with the recent past than is actually the case.[18] More particularly, Zygmunt Bauman's previously-mentioned notion of "liquid modernity" richly captures an essential feature of our late-modern world: incessant change—updating, avant-gardism, revision, innovation, emancipation, transformation—usually undertaken in the name of greater efficiency and/or for satisfying and expanding (and, alas, manufacturing) human desires.[19] While political and cultural drivers for this spirit are aplenty, Bauman compellingly identifies the exigencies of consumer capitalism as a principal agent.[20] In doing so, he follows Karl Marx, who, although he got many things tragically wrong, offered one of the most memorable descriptions of a market economy's convulsive capacity for creative destruction and innovation—a description that arguably applies better to our world than it did in the nineteenth century. In the *Communist Manifesto*, Marx and Engels wrote:

> Constant revolutionizing of production, uninterrupted disturbance of all social conditions, everlasting uncertainty and agitation distinguish the bourgeois epoch from all earlier ones. All fixed, fast-frozen relations, with their train of ancient and venerable prejudices and opinions, are swept away, all new-formed ones become antiquated before they can ossify. All that is solid melts into air, all that is holy is profaned, and man is at last compelled to

17. See Sajed, "Late Modernity/Postmodernity."

18. The strongest case for usage of *postmodernism* remains Lyotard's classic, *Postmodern Condition.*

19. On this point, see Gregory, *Unintended Reformation*, especially the chapter entitled, "Manufacturing the Goods Life."

20. Bauman, *Liquid Modernity*, 53–59.

face with sober senses his real conditions of life, and his relations with his kind.[21]

In Marx's day, this convulsive spirit was a radical novelty. In ours, it has become routinized. It is the air we breathe, the water we swim in. Ironically, it itself has become a tradition, and arguably *the* tradition of our times. As the sociologist James Davison Hunter observes: "A consumer mentality has moved out of the marketplace to become a dominant cultural logic [of our age], transforming inherited frameworks of moral meaning and social obligation."[22] But in such an environment, what is the fate of those "ancient and venerable prejudices," i.e., religious traditions, before the horizon of the coming decades of the twenty-first century? What questions do they now face, what challenges, what opportunities?

Ours is also an age of pluralism. Once upon a time, social theorists thought that "secularization" was the master narrative of the modern age. Under the influence of pioneering scholars such as August Comte, Emilé Durkheim, and Max Weber, social scientists in the middle decades of the twentieth century latched on to this concept—usually tagged as "secularization theory" or the "secularization thesis"—as the dominant paradigm for explaining social and intellectual changes wrought by modernization. Succinctly stated: as societies transitioned from the "traditional" (rural, hierarchical, religious) to the "modern," a process of secularization would reliably occur, incrementally undermining the plausibility and influence of religious commitment in institutions and individuals' consciousness.[23] In the 1990s, the sociologist Peter Berger (with others following him) famously defected from his guild, convinced that the global religious data simply did not support the secularization thesis as it had been handed down; he was also disturbed by how the idea was often presented in quasi-teleological terms as a "law" of modern history and how it led scholars to

---

21. Marx and Engels, *Communist Manifesto*, 222–23. Recently, an Uber driver called to my attention the fact that Uber, a radically innovative business, was founded at a moment when driverless cars already loomed as an industry-disrupting possibility. Recognizing the social and cultural turbulence of "creative destruction" should not be mistaken for nostalgia for a time before modern dentistry and modern plumbing. Peter Berger's *The Capitalist Revolution*—a balanced reckoning of the unprecedented human goods wrought by a market economy—is recommended reading for anyone given to unreflective vituperation against "capitalism" or "neoliberalism." See also Daniel Bell's classic, *The Cultural Contradictions of Capitalism*.

22. Hunter, *To Change the World*.

23. For a restatement of the secularization thesis, see Bruce, *Secularization*.

make assumptions about religion as a diminishing anachronism.[24] Yet in more recent years, and especially since 9/11, the term *post-secular* has come to signify a raging new interest in religion in the academy.[25]

To be sure, Berger and those who followed him made some exceptions. One might, for example, speak of political secularism, as David Novak and Ebrahim Moosa do in their contributions to this book, if one means simply tolerance, religious liberty, and/or church-state separation. But political secularism should not be mistaken for full-on cognitive secularism—a wholly "immanent frame," to use the language of Charles Taylor.[26] Concerning the latter, Berger admits that Western Europe and Western-educated intellectuals, grouped primarily in urban and educational centers around the globe, appears in aggregate more secular than religious in their thought. But these are the exceptions that confirmed the rule of perduringly religious societies throughout the world. This is true despite processes of modernization, which Berger compellingly defines as "the transformation in the human condition from fate to choice."[27] This transformation in turn owes its existence to prior, enormous changes in transportation, communication, literacy, education, free trade, and the rise of democratic forms of government that have taken place over the last few centuries.[28] Generally speaking, a child in twenty-first century Paris has prodigiously more "life options" than a child, say, in thirteenth-century Paris.

And these options include religious options or "preferences." In this sense, modernization has not been without significant effect on religious traditions worldwide, but "secularization" is perhaps not the most apt descriptor of these changes. A better descriptor is pluralism. "Modernity pluralizes," as Berger summarizes. People have more religious options, and, yes, now secular ones, too. "Modernization unleashes all the forces that make for pluralism—urbanization, mass migration (including tourism), general literacy, and higher education for increasing numbers, and all the recent technologies of communication. In our globalized modernity, almost everyone talks with everyone else. . . . [Most people] are aware

---

24. Gorski and Altinordu, "After Secularization?"

25. See, inter alia, Habermas, "Secularism's Crisis of Faith"; Branch, "Post-Secular Studies"; Blond, *Post-Secular Philosophy*.

26. Taylor, *Secular Age*, 539–93.

27. Berger, *Many Altars of Modernity*, 5.

28. Osterhammel, *Transformation of the World*.

of the fact that there are different ways of life, different values, different worldviews."[29] What is more, modernity/pluralism does not appear exactly the same in every country and region. No standard-issue modernity exists but rather what the Israeli sociologist Shmuel Eisenstadt has called "multiple modernities."[30] Although they might have some common features, modernity in Norway does not look as it does in Indonesia; in Qatar it differs from that of Belgium.[31] But in all cases, modernity has brought about a shift from relative cultural and religious homogeneity to relative cultural and religious heterogeneity—a social condition exacerbated by the aforementioned cultural logic of a consumer mentality, even if we might simultaneously regard this mentality as a common feature of (late) modern societies.[32]

In such a milieu, contributors to this volume were asked, how can a religious tradition be faithful to its highest principles? Can it thrive? Can it avoid the Scylla of mindlessly recoiling from modernity and the Charybdis of mindlessly accommodating to it? Or, in the words of David Novak in his chapter on Judaism and political modernity, how can it achieve a viable *tertium ad quid*?

The growing proximity of "religious others" to one another—and, sadly, the fear, extremism, and violence that has often erupted because of this—has been a major factor in the rise of Christian ecumenism and interreligious dialogue in the twentieth century.[33] Many theories and theologies about "dialogue" have concurrently arisen.[34] Some traditions—or at least sectors within them—have reacted skeptically to such dialogue, worried that its promotion only fosters religious relativism or syncretism. Sometimes such skepticism has not been warranted, but sometimes it has,

---

29. Berger, *Many Altars of Modernity*, 15. See also Berger, *Heretical Imperative*.

30. See Eisenstadt, *Multiple Modernities*.

31. Permit me to note that Qatar (with other Gulf States) has witnessed what can only be described as hyper-modernization in the past several decades combined with an implacable commitment to Sunni Islam among Qataris. See Fromherz, *Qatar*.

32. For a compelling popularization of Berger's thesis, see Micklethwait and Woolridge, *God Is Back*.

33. See Howard, *Faiths of Others*; Brodeur, "From the Margins to the Center"; Braybrooke, *Pilgrimage of Hope*; Sacks, *Not in God's Name*.

34. See, e.g., the various contributions in Cornille, *Wiley-Blackwell Companion to Inter-Religious Dialogue*. Arguably, the leading theorist of dialogue in the twentieth century was the Jewish philosopher Martin Buber. See Buber, "Dialogue." "The limits of the possibility of dialogue," Buber felicitously writes, "are the limits of awareness" (Buber, "Dialogue," 10).

especially given the widespread, beguiling bromide that all religions ultimately reflect or say "the same thing."[35] Recognizing this, we desired that our conference—and this book—offer a compelling example of dialogue, one to which people of different faiths—and whether conservative, liberal, or somewhere in-between—could ascribe to. To accomplish this aim, we thought it best to start closest to home with other Christians. Thus, while there is a Protestant (Lutheran) contributor, Sarah Hinlicky Wilson, we also welcomed the contributions of James L. Heft (Catholic) and David Bentley Hart (Orthodox), making this an ecumenical affair. But we did not stop there. We ventured out to other religious neighbors—those from the "Abrahamic" faith traditions—hence the inclusion of David Novak (Jewish) and Ebrahim Moosa (Muslim). Finally, we alighted on a topic of common concern—maintaining a tradition in our late-modern age—rather than discussing predictably neuralgic interfaith issues, such as the person of Christ or the Trinity and the like.

Of course, many voices are not represented here—those from South Asian religious traditions, for example—but also more proximate voices, Mennonites, Presbyterians, Methodists, Mormons, among others. If one had world enough and time (and money!), we would have happily included more. But one must begin somewhere, and I humbly submit that the material presented here, although limited in scope, in fact has much broader relevance for various religious traditions in their multifarious efforts to understand and negotiate the social and cultural currents of late modernity.

This volume does not seek to advance any particular theology or theory of ecumenism or interreligious dialogue. Still, it merits mentioning that I have found inspiration and insight from two key documents of the Second Vatican Council (1962–65). The first is its "Decree on Ecumenism" (*Unitatis redintegratio*), promulgated in 1965. It encouraged Catholics to seek out "separated brethren" and "prudently and patiently" come into conversation with them in a spirit of irenicism, friendship, and cooperation, adding: "Today, in many parts of the world, under the inspiring grace of

---

35. For a forceful criticism of this bromide from a "postliberal" theological respective, see George Lindbeck's classic work, *The Nature of Doctrine*. Lindbeck is especially critical of the notion that all religions are simply expressions of some common core of human experience. Those who begin with this premise, he argues, are forced into the quandary of having to evaluate which religions are superior and which are inferior expressions of this common experience. By contrast, dialogue partners who assume that religions are "simply different can proceed to explore their agreements and disagreements without necessarily engaging in the invidious comparisons that the assumption of a common experiential core makes so tempting" (Lindbeck, *Nature of Doctrine*, 55).

the Holy Spirit, many efforts are being made in prayer, word, and action to attain that fullness of unity which Jesus Christ desires. The Sacred Council exhorts . . . [the] faithful to recognize the signs of the times and to take an active and intelligent part in the work of ecumenism."[36]

The Second Vatican Council also endorsed interreligious dialogue in its groundbreaking document, *Nostra aetate*, the "Declaration on the Relation of the Church to Non-Christian Religions" (1965).[37] It "exhorts her [the Church's] sons, that through dialogue and collaboration with the followers of other religions, carried out with prudence and love and in witness to the Christian faith and life, they recognize, preserve, and promote the good things, spiritual and moral, as well as the socio-cultural values found among these men." Furthermore, while recognizing the abiding and often insuperable differences among religious traditions, *Nostra aetate* made clear that the Catholic Church "rejects nothing that is true and holy" in other faith traditions.[38] Put differently, the maintenance of honest and deeply-held disagreements among different believers does not preclude admiring and even learning from one another. To deny these differences suggests dishonesty; to over-emphasize them, quarrelsomeness.

Because of their historical and theological proximity to Christianity, Judaism and Islam occupy prominent positions in *Nostra aetate*. A young theological consultant at Vatican II, Pope John Paul II once even referred to Judaism as Christianity's "elder brother in the faith."[39] In *Nostra aetate*, the Catholic Church rued past expressions of anti-Judaism, decrying "hatred, persecutions, displays of anti-Semitism, directed against Jews at any time and by anyone." "Since the spiritual patrimony common to Christians and Jews is thus so great," it goes on to say, "this sacred synod wants to foster and recommend . . . mutual understanding and respect . . . [and] fraternal dialogues" between the two faiths.[40]

With respect to Islam, *Nostra aetate* had this to say: "The Church regards with esteem also Muslims. They adore the one God, living and subsisting in Himself; merciful and all-powerful, the Creator of heaven and

36. Flannery, *Vatican II*, 452–70.

37. For an overview of its genesis and impact, see O'Collins, *Second Vatican Council on Other Religions*, 84–108; Pratt, *Church and Other Faiths*, 167–82.

38. Flannery, *Vatican II*, 738–42.

39. John Paul II, *Crossing the Threshold of Faith*, 99.

40. Flannery, *Vatican II*, 740–42. To understand *Nostra aetate* in a larger historical framework, see Connelly, *From Enemy to Brother*; Oesterreicher, *New Encounter*.

earth, who has spoken to men; they take pains to submit wholeheartedly to even His inscrutable decrees, just as Abraham, with whom the faith of Islam takes pleasure in linking itself, submitted to God. . . . Since in the course of centuries not a few quarrels and hostilities have arisen between Christians and Muslims, this sacred synod urges all . . . [to] work sincerely for mutual understanding and to preserve as well as to promote together for the benefit of all mankind social justice and moral welfare, as well as peace and freedom."[41] In our post-9/11 world, these words are more relevant than ever, and implementing them requires charity, prudence, and good will.

To be sure, much more could be said about these documents and their reception in the late twentieth and twenty-first centuries, among Catholics and those from other traditions.[42] Suffice it to say, however, that our humble conference, in a historically Lutheran environment, took no small measure of inspiration from the words of the Council, which recently marked its own fiftieth anniversary. It should not be lost on anyone, moreover, that these documents themselves—and our "Protestant" appropriation of them—represent noteworthy examples of religious traditions grappling with their own past, rethinking aspects of them, and attempting to make them salient and alive in the present without vitiating or diluting what has been handed down. Or, in the frequently-invoked watchwords of Vatican II, these endeavors constitute examples of *ressourcement* (returning to the tradition for insight) for the purpose of *aggiornamento* (engaging with present-day realities).[43]

***

Offering summaries of chapters is always a perilous undertaking, because much necessarily must be left out. Still, to give the reader some sense of what to expect in the pages ahead, permit me, briefly, to offer synopses of each chapter.

In chapter 1, "Tradition or Innovation as the Dilemma of Modern Judaism," David Novak argues that Jews, like other religious communities,

---

41. Flannery, *Vatican II*, 739–40 (translation modified). For the broader context of this statement, see Siddiqui, *Christian-Muslim Dialogue*. On efforts by and challenges to interfaith dialogue among Muslims, see Kayaoglu, "Explaining Interfaith Dialogue."

42. On its reception, see Faggioli, *Council for a Global Church*; Lamb and Levering, *Reception of Vatican II*.

43. See Lamb and Levering, *Vatican II*, 5.

have often had a difficult time coming to terms with modernity, even as it has also presented opportunities. Since the French Revolution (1789), Jews have gained rights as individuals—i.e., as citizens of pluralistic, modern states—even as they have lost many prerogatives as a community that was once prevalent in the legal orders of the Old Regime. At the onset of the modern era, Novak argues, one witnessed two very different Jewish responses to this novel reality. On one hand, Moses Mendelssohn (1729–86) embraced modernity: Jews should welcome giving up their communal rights to gain them as individual citizens. In other words, they should be fully part of the modern state. Conversely, Rabbi Moses Schreiber (1762–1839) stridently condemned modernity, arguing that in order to protect the purity of the faith, Jews should keep themselves apart from the modern state. But what if both being "part of" and being "apart from" miss the mark, as Novak asks? The chapter argues that there is yet a third way: Jews should be "participants in" the modern state even as they recognize that this participation is ultimately subordinate to their highest loyalties, which are reserved for God alone as mediated through Jewish Scripture and tradition. Lessons from the book of Esther, Novak points out, offer guidance in helping envision what this model of participation ought to look like in our own day and age.

In his contribution, "Tradition: A Catholic Understanding," Father James L. Heft, OM, a leading Catholic educator and theologian, argues that for a robust Catholic tradition to be maintained and extended into the future, a healthy relationship must exist among bishops, academic theologians, and the laity. In both past and present, that relationship has been jeopardized, he feels, often by bishops too eager to exercise authority unilaterally, neither consulting with theologians nor with the faithful on matters concerning faith, practice, and worship. This chapter argues that the thought of John Henry Newman and the experience of the Second Vatican Council offer instruction in how to achieve a healthy back-and-forth among these three parties. The notion of *sensus fidelium*—the wisdom gained by the laity in their efforts to live out the faith on a daily basis—is especially significant, Heft maintains.[44] Bishops must take it into consideration and converse with theologians—and the academy at large, Tertullian's "Athens"—as they chart a future course for the Church in our late-modern world.[45] Admittedly, concord among these three parties has

44. On this notion, see Hartlin, "*Sensus Fidelium*"; Kirk, *Sensus Fidelium*.

45. Permit me also to note that problems arise when religiously observant academics

never come easily, and the best that might be achieved is a creative tension among them. Yet this is the path that the Catholic Church must choose, Heft argues. The Church must even robustly embrace these tensions accompanied by the virtue of hope and under the guidance of the Holy Spirit. In this way, a living tradition—and not an ossified traditionalism—can be sustained.

In his chapter, the Orthodox theologian and polemicist David Bentley Hart takes a witty swipe at those, upset by modernity, given to romanticizing the past uncritically. But he has little patience with John Henry Newman's notion of "development"—something Heft refers to quite approvingly.[46] Instead, Hart argues that for the Christian tradition to retain its vitality, it must always be in touch with its "initiating moment," its "animating impulse," the forces that gave it life and shape in the first place. In the course of history, doctrines, councils, and creeds may very well be necessary, but in light of the faith's aboriginal, kairotic verities, these will always be limited and contingent phenomena, opening new theological questions and insights even if they might close old ones. The "secret" or "hidden" drama of these verities working themselves out over time, Hart contrasts with "bare history," modernity's dreary march of profane consecutive moments: time divested of sacred meaning and purpose. The former drama is in fact our true history, a spiritual epic still in the making, known fully by God alone, and which we might only glimpse as through a glass darkly.

In his chapter, "Disruptions and Connections: Rediscovering and Remaking Muslim Tradition in Late Modernity," Notre Dame's Ebrahim Moosa, a Muslim and a leading authority on medieval and modern Islam, makes clear that the question of tradition is at the forefront of both politics and theology throughout the Muslim world today. Sadly, he notes that sometimes passions are sufficiently high and positions polarized to "preclude coherent conversation." "Contemporary Islam in its multiple struggles for the reappropriation of tradition," he notes, "has [had] to deal with the fate of [modern] history and a world altered by . . . Western colonialism and the fragmentation of the Muslim world into nation-states."[47] He worries about

feel that they only relate to their religious communities in a spirit of "prophetic" leadership, seeing themselves self-assuredly as guides, never as learners. On this point, see Meilaender, "Conscience and Authority."

46. See Newman, *Essay on the Development of Christian Doctrine*, first published in 1845.

47. This verbiage comes from Moosa's original conference paper; it is modified slightly in the chapter that follows.

those who desire simply to escape modernity into hidebound conformity with an imagined past (*taqlid* in Arabic), and he especially regrets those intellectuals, such as the late Saba Mahmood, who have been overeager to interpret some reformist voices within Islam as dupes of Western (especially US) foreign policy. Instead, to find a way forward, contemporary Muslim scholars, while also engaging with present-day voices, ought to return to a towering figure in their own intellectual tradition: Ibn Khaldun (1332–1406). They must go imaginatively back in order to go promisingly forward—a virtual refrain in calls for renewal within religious traditions. Khaldun's thought, Moosa believes, provides patterns of interpretation and categories of understanding to help Muslims today distinguish between better and worse, more rational and less rational, understandings of their tradition. In following Khaldun, Moosa feels that Islam has a chance for genuine, thoughtful renewal, avoiding being rigidly beholden to tradition (or modern absolutized versions of it) on the one hand and "selling out" completely to modernity on the other.

Finally, the Lutheran pastor and editor of *Lutheran Forum*, Sarah Hinlicky Wilson, describes tradition bluntly as "simply the ability to think," since we are all creatures of time and inheritors of that which came before us. In her chapter, "Tradition: A Lutheran Point of View," she takes up three abidingly relevant challenges facing practitioners within a tradition in our era of "accelerating modernity." In the first, she examines the movement of a tradition across cultural and national boundaries—from Europe to Africa and especially to India—and how thinkers within a tradition must discriminate between life-giving adaptations and additions versus syncretic and possibly fatal compromises. Second, she pursues the challenge of a tradition facing questions never before asked and seeking answers within its own resources never before put to such uses—this time, looking at the issue of women's public discourse in the church. The final section tackles the difficulty of recognizing a morally irredeemable aspect of a tradition—in this instance, Christian anti-Judaism—and how practitioners of a tradition might excise it, deploying theological resources from the very same tradition in the process.

As should be clear, no uniform vision of tradition is presented in the chapters that follow. Each author has interpreted the initial mandate and set of questions given to them in light of their own theological standpoint and from their respective areas of scholarly competence and interest. Different approaches have resulted, although at times certain echoes will become heard as will conflicting points of view. No attempt has been made to resolve the latter. It is the more modest hope of the editor and contributors alike that the attentive reader will simply find much to reflect on with respect to the "Abrahamic" religious traditions: their past, present, and possible futures in the cultural and social milieux of late modernity. It is additionally hoped that such reflections will help us all discern the truth of our world more insightfully and equip us to love our neighbors more steadfastly.

1

Tradition or Innovation
as the Dilemma of Modern Judaism

David Novak
University of Toronto

INTRODUCTION: POLITICAL STATUS OF THE JEWS: OLD AND NEW

The question of how tradition and innovation are related is certainly one that contemporary Jewish thinkers have to confront regularly. In order to understand its true importance, though, we need to see how it arose at the very dawn of modernity (at least for Jews), namely, in late eighteenth- and early nineteenth-century Europe. Indeed, one can see the question raised most starkly by the liberal nobleman, Count Stanislas de Clermont Tonnerre, in a speech to the French National Assembly on December 23, 1789, when he asserted: "Everything is to be refused to the Jews as a nation; everything is to be granted to the Jews as individuals" (*Il faut tout refuser aux Juifs comme nation, et accorder tout aux Juifs comme individus*).[1] Now designating "the Jews as a nation" means the way European Jews were constituted politically by the *ancien régime* and by themselves, namely, as a semi-independent community (a *qahal* in rabbinic terms) within a larger

1. https://fr.wikiquote.org/wiki/Stanislas_de_clermont-Tonnerre.

more independent polity (*imperium in imperio* or, in Tonnerre's words, *une nation dans la nation*), that larger polity enjoying fuller political liberty and wielding greater political power. (Tonnerre recalled their previous status as *un corps politique*.)[2] The smaller, more politically-dependent Jewish community was largely governed by rabbis as the official custodians, transmitters, interpreters, and applicators of the normative Jewish tradition (*masoret Israel* in rabbinic terms). The normativity of this tradition is believed to be rooted in "the Torah Moses accepted from God at Sinai."[3]

Most importantly, premodern (or "mediaeval") European Jews did not take their theological-political warrant from the Christian regime hosting them; instead, their warrant came from the Torah God revealed to Israel at Sinai, which the Jewish tradition deems to be the official vehicle of its normative transmission. Indeed, the Christian host regime also took its theological-political warrant from the Torah the same God revealed to Israel at Sinai *plus* (i.e., as *novum testamentum*) the Torah God revealed to Israel at Sinai as embodied in Christ. Therefore, both Jews and Christians had to find authorizations within their own respective, revelation-based traditions for entering into a political relationship with one another in good faith.[4]

In this premodern situation, the political arrangement of Jews in Christendom was not a relationship of individual Jews and the non-Jewish host state; instead, a relationship between the Jewish community (where one's status therein was a largely *natal* or "national" matter) and the Christian regime pertained. The standards that governed this political relationship and the status of the Jews in it were negotiated through a contract between the non-Jewish sovereign and the foreign Jewish nation living in his or her domain under their rule. Conversely, though, in the modern regime Clermont Tonnerre was advocating (very much influenced by Rousseau's *Le contrat social*), the political relationship was to be between *all* individual citizens and the state. As such, the modern state so conceived had to revoke the traditional communal rights of the church as much as it had to revoke the traditional communal rights of the Jewish community.

In fact, the revocation of the traditional communal rights of the church was more radical than the revocation of the traditional communal rights of the Jewish nation, since the church under the *ancien régime* provided the

2. For more background, see Hertzberg, *French Enlightenment and the Jews*.

3. *Avot* 1:1.

4. For further discussion of these points, see Novak, *Jewish Social Contract*.

theological warrant for the state itself, by which the state permitted only Christians to be first-class citizens. (In fact, many poorer Christians were third-class serfs, under the control of the aristocracy, and in many ways, theirs was an even more precarious existence than that of the Jews.) All Christians in the realm were first members of *the* church and the subjects of *a* Christian sovereign subsequently. (This theological-political reality is best expressed in the famous words of Thomas More to King Henry VIII on the occasion of his martyr's death on July 6, 1535, declaring himself to be "the King's good servant but God's first."[5]) Jews could only be second-class, tolerated aliens in this kind of regime unless, of course, they converted to Christianity and ceased to be Jewish. Such conversion to Christianity meant exchanging their ancient religio-political status within a minority community for a newer religio-political status within the majority community. For Jews as for Christians, such an existential move could only be regarded as apostasy, although Jews did not have the political power to pursue Jewish apostates the way Christians could pursue Christian apostates—to forcibly bring them back under the church's control. Nevertheless, both Judaism and Christianity teach that if apostasy is forced upon one, that person should choose to die a martyr's death in its stead.

After the French Revolution, Jews could now become full citizens of the state without apostasy.[6] Moreover, Jews were able to accept their new status in the modern state more easily than Christians could accept their new status there. To be sure, most Jews in Western Europe (i.e., those countries affected by the French Revolution) regarded modernity as being their political and even cultural gain, while most Christians regarded modernity as being their political and even cultural loss. In Western democracies like the United States and Canada, where even though these states have never been officially "Christian" in the legal or political sense, Christians still have enjoyed the cultural hegemony of the majority. Yet these Christians are now suffering the loss of something the Jews have never had. The Jews gained political power they didn't have as a community while Christians lost the political power they did have as a community, i.e., as the dominant community in Western polities. This might explain why Christians who long for Christendom as their idealized *ancien régime* at times turn into

---

5. More quoted in Chambers, *Thomas More*, 349. The often volatile relationship between crown and altar in medieval Christendom is most powerfully dramatized by T. S. Eliot in "Murder in the Cathedral."

6. For some of the historical terrain to which I am alluding, see Elon, *Pity of It All.*

anti-modern anti-Semites, resentful of the power that they believe the Jews have taken for themselves in modernity at the expense of Christians.

SOCIAL CONTRACT: OLD AND NEW

The acquisition of this new political power by modern Jews can be seen as based on the newer modern notion of the social contract. It is very much different from the premodern notion of the social contract, which we have been examining. The old social contract was a negotiated agreement between two national communities, each of whose rulers received their traditional political warrant from God's covenant with their community. The revealed constitution of the community is written and preserved in a book (i.e., a *sefer* in Hebrew; *biblos* in Greek, hence "the Bible"), then transmitted (*masoret* in Hebrew; *traditio* in Latin) to and through the community intergenerationally, i.e., historically. (The biblical term *toldot* or "generations," as in Genesis 5:1, in modern Hebrew becomes "history."[7]) As revelation itself is an event *in* history, so is tradition a process moving with revelation's content *through* history, towards the end of history, as a hoped for eschatological end as yet unknown to any creature.[8] As such, the parties to the premodern social contract came to the contract with considerable traditional baggage, which they not only wanted to keep but also wanted the social contract to protect and even help flourish. In no way did they want to cede their ultimate existential commitment to the new state created by the social contract; in fact, they didn't have to do so.

The newly contracted state of affairs (*status civilis*) was not taken to be the kingdom of God on earth nor even a facsimile thereof. (The old covenanted community, conversely, is considered to be those waiting for the kingdom and their redemption, although not claiming to provide it themselves.) Contrast this with the view of the most prominent and influential twentieth-century social contract theorist, John Rawls, who insisted that individuals coming to the social contract do so from behind what he calls "a veil of ignorance," meaning that all the individual parties to the social contract are to permanently leave behind all their "comprehensive conceptions of the good" (which, in most cases, are derived from traditionally religious

7. For the difference between classical Jewish "remembrance" and modern Jewish "history," see Yerushalmi, *Zakhor.*

8. See 1 Cor 2:9; *Berakhot* 34b (cf. Isa 64:3).

sources).[9] Therefore, the hallmark of modernity, in this view anyway, is the notion that our most fundamental political arrangements are made *de novo*, i.e., they are made in direct opposition to any binding commitment to our respective traditions. Modernity is essentially innovative or dynamic; tradition is essentially conservative or static. In this view, "never the twain shall meet." For those of this modernist mindset, modernity is essentially anti-tradition. That is because heteronomy or autonomy is presupposed by two very different kinds of society.

AUTONOMY IN PLACE OF HETERONOMY

What exactly do I mean by this?

Modernists think our respective traditions are essentially "heteronomous." That is true in the sense that traditional authority comes from the revelation of a transcendent God. Conversely, modernity emphasizes "autonomy," i.e., human self-creation (almost *ex nihilo*).[10] Yet the autonomy emphasized by secular modernity is not the autonomy of individual wills (as it is for Locke). Instead, it is much more Rousseau's "general will" (*volonté générale*), into which the will of each individual (*volonté particulière*) merges collectively, i.e., after it has divested itself of all connection to the collective authority of any ancient tradition. (Social critic Harold Rosenberg once called this kind of autonomy the worldview of "the herd of independent minds."[11]) Thus modern autonomy is just as collective as the traditional heteronomy it claims to have overthrown, even if the rhetoric of modernity seems to suggests that this is not the case.

Now tradition's collective authority is only valid when rooted in and stemming from revelation. Indeed, the "other" (i.e., the *heteros* of *heteronomy*) who founds the traditional community by means of election could only be God as *Deus revelatus*. Without that foundational commitment to revelation, a tradition becomes escapist nostalgia, hiding from or fighting against innovative modernity rather than being able to engage it from a transcendent perspective. The question to be squarely faced by Jews and Christians (and now possibly by Western Muslims, too) is how to adhere

9. Rawls, *Theory of Justice*, 118–23; *Political Liberalism*, 216–26. For a trenchant critique of Rawls on these very points, see Goodman, *Religious Pluralism*, 54–101.

10. For the most comprehensive study of this crucial modern idea, see Schneewind, *Invention of Autonomy*.

11. Rosenberg, *Discovering the Present*, 25–28.

to our respective revelation-based traditions neither (in the words of our editor) "mindlessly recoiling from modernity" nor "mindlessly accommodating to it." Along these lines, let me suggest a point I hope to develop a bit later in this chapter, namely, that there is a third conceptual term (*tertium quid*) that might well resolve the seeming impasse between immutable tradition and mutable modernity, i.e., between "medieval" heteronomy and modern autonomy; and this resolution does not require us to reject one conception in favor of the other. Before that, though, let us look at two important early modern advocates of these opposing conceptions, whose influences are still found in contemporary or late-modern Judaism.

The most important early modern advocate of modernity was the Enlightenment Jewish philosopher, Moses Mendelssohn (d. 1786). As the chief spokesman for the political emancipation of the Jews in Prussia, Mendelssohn had to argue against the charge of the opponents of Jewish emancipation that the Jews could not be citizens of a democratic state in good faith, even one that did not require their conversion to Christianity as the price of admission to full citizenship in the new "secular" state (in Europe, secular *de facto* if not yet *de jure*).[12] That was because the fundamental political commitment of the Jews is to their "nation." As such, Jews could not become equals of the other citizens of the state, who have transferred their former fundamental political commitment to the church now to the state. (Of course, this argument could more easily be made in Protestant Prussia than in Catholic Bavaria.)

Although a fully traditional Jew in his own personal life, Mendelssohn argued to both Jews and gentiles that the Jews were ready to give up their communal rights in order to become individual citizens of the state. The traditional religion of the Jews, i.e., "Judaism," could now become the ideology of a private, voluntary association of like-minded practitioners of the Jewish tradition, especially its "revealed legislation" (*Halakhah* in Hebrew), which primarily meant uniquely Jewish religious practices, like the Sabbath and dietary restrictions. To use German terminology already familiar in Mendelssohn's time, the Jews were to comprise a *Gesellschaft*

---

12. Mendelssohn's main statement of his religio-political philosophy is Mendelssohn, *Jerusalem*. The most comprehensive treatment of Mendelssohn's intertwined life and thought is Altmann, *Moses Mendelssohn*. For a critique of Mendelssohn's religio-political philosophy, especially as it pertains to Judaism, see Novak, *Jewish Social Contract*, 164–69. For a more sympathetic treatment of Mendelssohn's philosophy, especially as it pertains to Judaism, see Sacks, *Moses Mendelssohn's Living Script*.

or "society" rather than a *Gemeinschaft* or "community."[13] While not being fully overcome by modernity, ancient Jewish tradition was now clearly subordinated to the secular state. While retaining its religious or "ritual" independence, Judaism was now to cede the moral/political authority it once had to the state. This point had precedence in the Jewish heretic Baruch Spinoza's *Tractatus Theologico-Politicus* as well as in his *Tractatus Politicus*. However well intended, this was not a reconciliation of tradition and innovative modernity as much as it was a surrender of tradition to innovative modernity—with the faint hope that the state would not interfere in the strictly ritual affairs of the Jews. It is little wonder, then, that the liberal Jews who looked to Mendelssohn as their forerunner quickly altered their ritual practices to be more in line with those of the Euro-centric majority, and thus not stand out as being "foreign" or "oriental."

Now when the moral consensus of the society was fairly consistent with the Jewish tradition, liberal Jews (and liberal Christians) did not really have to change their traditional morality to be consistent with secular morality. However, today, when secular morality is more and more at odds with traditional Jewish (and Christian, hence "Judeo-Christian") morality, were Moses Mendelssohn alive today, I think he would be enough of a faithful Jew to oppose both the ritual and moral innovations of liberal Judaism. Nevertheless, there is little if anything in his optimistic view of the essential compatibility of the Jewish tradition and secular modernity that could give him (or anybody following him) any good reasons to cogently oppose these moral innovations, which are now often seen as radical rejections of the Jewish moral tradition per se.

Unlike Mendelssohn's time, when secular morality was still quite similar to its origins in the Bible, much of secular morality today no longer looks to traditional Judeo-Christian morality as precedent to be invoked; instead, it looks upon that traditional morality as immorality to be overcome, especially on such issues as marriage, parenthood, abortion, and euthanasia. Indeed, many contemporary secularists recognize quite clearly that their prime enemy is the theological anthropology of the Bible that teaches human persons are the "image of God" (*imago Dei*). Most of them follow the nineteenth-century philosopher Ludwig Feuerbach (who inspired both Marx and Freud), who argued that, in fact, God is the idealized self that humans have projected onto reality. Once human beings become

---

13. For the locus classicus on this distinction in modern social science, see Tönnies, *Community and Association.*

aware of what they have done unconsciously, they should drop any consideration of a relationship with the by now nonexistent God, regarded as an illusion due to their philosophical enlightenment.

The moral corollary of this biblical anthropology is that we humans ought to interact with each other *like* God interacts with us (*imitatio Dei*). This connection between *what* we humans essentially *are* and *how* we *ought* to interact with each other is seen in the rabbinic treatment of the biblical teaching that God creates humans "in our image [*be-tsalmenu*] according to our likeness [*ke-demutenu*] (Gen 1:26). But what is the difference between "image" and "likeness"? It might be said that being made in God's image tells human beings that we have the unique creaturely capacity to be intimately related to God inasmuch as we are taught God loves us. As one ancient Rabbi put it: "Beloved [*haviv*] are humans [*adam*] who are created in the image, and even more beloved are those to whom it has been made known [in Scripture]."[14] Only because of that are we able to love God back responsively.[15] Now that intimate relationship with God can only be conducted in our traditional communities, who can respond to God's love positively only because it has been revealed to us in our singular historical interactions with God and we are able to re-experience that love in our active commemoration of those events.[16] Nevertheless, God's love is neither confined to our traditional communities nor is it only with certain exalted individual human persons.[17] That love coming from God to us ought to include all those who are our human neighbors in the world, whether they recognize the source of that love or not.[18] Thus our task in the world is to *be like* God in our loving interactions with each other, with whomever. As one ancient Rabbi taught: "Just as God is gracious and compassionate, so shall you be gracious and compassionate."[19]

All of this theological anthropology and its moral corollaries are suspect and increasingly not even tolerated by modern dogmatic secularists. Although Mendelssohn cannot be blamed for what followed in his wake, I cannot find in his thought any antidote to it either. Thus he has little to

14. *Avot* 3:18 (cf. Gen 9:6).

15. *Shabbat* 133b (cf. Exod 15:2).

16. This is emphasized by the great medieval theologian Nahmanides (d. 1270) in his Torah commentary. See Novak, *Theology of Nahmanides*, 116–17.

17. See Amos 9:7.

18. *Gittin* 61a.

19. *Shabbat* 133b (cf. Exod 34:6).

offer to those opposing the notion that innovative modernity continually trumps religious traditions, based as they are on what is now taken to be a fantasy or an illusion about a God who never existed or whom modernity has successfully killed. As the ancient pagan philosopher Lucretius put it: "From nothing, nothing comes" (*ex nihilo nihil fit*).[20]

AUTONOMY OVER HETERONOMY

Mendelssohn's antithesis was Rabbi Moses Schreiber (d. 1839), the founder of what came to be called "Orthodox Judaism," which might also be called the Jewish "Counterreformation."[21] (I say "counterreformation" since, in the nineteenth century, Liberal Judaism began calling itself "Reform Judaism"—in Protestant Prussia—and the main type of liberal Judaism today still calls itself by that name.) In his opposition to Reform Judaism, which he saw as innovation for innovation's sake, Schreiber adopted as his slogan the Talmudic rule: "What is new is forbidden by the Torah" (*hadash asur min ha-torah*). (Actually, this Talmudic rule deals with a specific matter of Jewish agricultural law, so Schreiber's use of it as a general principle is metaphorical, not literal.[22]) Also, to be fair, when it came to some new issues confronting his own traditional or orthodox community (and those, mostly East European Jewish communities that looked to his religious leadership), Schreiber was occasionally innovative, although always couching his innovations in massive citations of the traditional literary sources of Jewish law. (We might compare this to the Catholic notion of *ressourcement* mentioned by Heft in his chapter.) His carefully argued and meticulous, precedent-citing innovations were at times thought to be necessary because of changing external circumstances, but they were never thought to be desirable per se. For Schreiber, modernity was a dangerous threat, not an attractive challenge. Thus Schreiber's acolytes derisively called all those who seemed to be innovating for its own sake "reformers" or "self-inventors" (*mithadshim*, literally "those who make themselves new"). If not actual apostasy, such innovativeness is considered heresy by Orthodox Jews in Schreiber's mold. It is to be vigorously opposed within the community. (This can be compared to the wholesale denunciation of "modernism" by Pope Pius X in his 1907 encyclical, *Pascendi dominici gregis*.)

20. Lucretius, *De Rerum Natura* 1.148–56.
21. See Skolnik and Berenbaum, *Encyclopedia Judaica*, 18:742–43, s.v. "Sofer, Moses."
22. *Orlah* 3:9.

Now the innovations Schreiber opposed were not just in such "ritual" matters as liturgical reform. Much more important for him as a "master of Halakhah" was the fallout from the French Revolution on the theological-political situation of the Jewish community. As the rabbi of a large, still very traditional Jewish community (in the still very traditional, very Catholic Austrian Empire), Schreiber was keenly aware that the political emancipation of the Jews (especially in France and, increasingly so, in the German states) meant the loss of communal authority of the Jewish tradition and of the rabbis as its traditionally empowered interpreters and enforcers. In other words, modernity represented a sea change, touching all social spheres, to the traditional Jewish imagination.

OVERCOMING THE IMPASSE OF HETERONOMY

Today, in our late-modern world, we are living on the other side of the changes wrought by modernity. And the question presents itself: how does one overcome the seeming impasse between Mendelssohn's subjugation of tradition to innovative modernity and Schreiber's subjugation of innovative modernity to tradition? Yet before proposing a *tertium quid* to accomplish this, we need to look at why neither Mendelssohn (*et alia*) and Schreiber (*et alia*) could not and would not accommodate the position of the other in some sort of dialectical balance. In fact, Schreiber at times attacked Mendelssohn by name. (Schreiber, who was only twenty-three years old when Mendelssohn died, was probably unknown to Mendelssohn.)

The key to understanding the limitations of both Mendelssohn's liberalism and Schreiber's orthodoxy might be found in their views of the relation of Jews to the surrounding secular world and, especially, to the secular state. For Mendelssohn, that relationship is the inclusion of individual citizens, whether Jewish or gentile, within the state as a *part of* the whole. For Schreiber, Jews are to keep themselves *apart from* the secular world as much as possible in order to preserve the purity of the faith. Unless there is some immediate political or economic advantage for the traditional community to deal with the secular state as an essentially occupying power, he no doubt wished the Jewish people could live without it altogether. Nevertheless, Schreiber was enough of a realist to tie that wish to the traditional Jewish hope for ultimate messianic redemption from any non-Jewish (and even liberal Jewish) rule.

However, there is a third kind of relation to the secular world that might provide us with the *tertium quid* we are seeking. What if instead of being a *part of* the secular state and society, and what if instead of being *apart from* them, Jews are to look upon themselves as *participants in* this world? But what makes being a participant-in different (and better) from being a part-of or apart-from? To borrow a well known adage, "one is to be *in* the world, not *of* it"; but let me adapt the adage to now say, "one is to participate in the secular state, yet neither be a part of it nor be apart from it."

The ability to be a participant-in rather than a part-of or apart-from the surrounding secular state and society depends on the type of constantly innovating secular state surrounding one. To be fair to both Mendelssohn and Schreiber, the kind of states surrounding them were fast becoming the kind of absolutist regimes where an either/or was the only possibility. One could only be part of it *or* apart from it. In fact, though, the innovative democracy Rousseau envisioned became just as absolutist, just as all-encompassing, as the traditional monarchy he sought to obliterate along with all other traditions. (Rousseau was the chief philosophical influence on the French Revolution and *laïcité*, the dogmatic secularism that still dominates Western European society, which many US and Canadian elites would also like to dominate our society.) One is either *for it/of it* or one is *apart from it/against it*. Indeed, the modern secular nation-state often promises this-worldly salvation, which can only be accepted *in toto* or rejected *in toto*. The moral authority of the state here is meant to be total therefore.[23]

The way out of this impasse is to deny that the secular state has this kind of ultimate authority. Surely, the United States and Canada are secular states insofar as they do not take their legitimating warrant from any religious tradition and its founding revelation. Moreover, at their best, they do not try to create a substitute for the religious/communal traditions of their citizens in the guise of "secularism" (the exception in Canada being ultra-nationalist Québecois ideologues). Hence, citizens are free to seek their ultimate commitments in traditions that historically long predate and ontologically transcend what ought to be the limited democratic state. Those of us who come from and still live by these pre-political traditions can cogently be *in* the state but never *of* it (like assimilationists). Moreover, we want to not only take *from* the state the protection of our rights (like even separatist sectarians do) but also to contribute *to* the state's flourishing

---

23. On the more radical notion of secularism implied by the French term *laïcité*, see Baubérot, "Secularization, Secularism, and Laïcité"; Berlinerblau, *Secularism on the Edge*.

as loyal citizens. That is because a truly limited democratic state is one that is actually more limited by our revelation-based traditions than it limits them. This limits the presumption of the state from exercising divine-like authority. When the state is less presumptive, though, we adherents of these traditions should encourage the state in its legitimate work in this world. Only when this is understood by a goodly number of citizens in this kind of state does the state and the civil society on which it depends become the best pluralistic environment for our Jewish and Christian traditions—and all other democracy-friendly traditions—to thrive in a changing world.

We can be truly critical citizens as participants in the secular state because our respective traditions provide us with a transcendent perspective from which to judge which of the state's policies are consistent with the universally applicable norms of the traditionally transmitted law of God, and which directly contradict it. That is, which public policies can we support in good faith, and which ones must we oppose? (However, those norms of God's law only applying to the covenanted community, such as the Sabbath and Festivals, are not criteria by which we require consistency from the state's public policies; instead, all we ask is that the state not prevent us from keeping them.) Moreover, like the biblical prophets, our critical stance towards the state is neither to regard it as our enemy (as sectarian separatists do) nor obsequiously become its servant (as assimilationists do) but rather to help and encourage the state and its society as their true and faithful friend. But we can only be that kind of friend in a genuinely multicultural society in which what we have to offer will not be ignored or scorned simply because it originates from religious considerations but where it stands a reasonably good chance of actually being accepted.

LEARNING FROM MODERNITY

Furthermore, we adherents of revelation-based traditions should not only *take from* the secular democratic state and its society what we need from it *for* our own communal survival, we should also *bring into* our traditional communities what we have learned from our experience in the world— from the various religious traditions present in the modern pluralistic state.

It seems to me that the most important thing we have learned from our experience here in democracies is that membership in any society, secular or religious, is best when it is voluntary rather than coerced. So, since membership in a secular democratic state is voluntary, citizens have the duty to obey the authority of the state and its laws because they have freely accepted that authority (whether tacitly or overtly). Nevertheless, citizens also have the right to question the state with impunity when they have grave doubts about its moral authority. Think here of Martin Luther King Jr. and the civil rights movement. That means, in fact, that the state and its society must regularly engage in the task of persuading its citizens of its rational, beneficent governance of all of them, thus encouraging each of them to remain loyal participants in the state and thereby discouraging their departure from it. (That is regularly done through parliamentary debate on laws to be passed and by regular plebiscites, when, it is hoped, citizens have the opportunity to vote for candidates for public office because of the policy proposals and the reasons by which they have argued for them.)

To be sure, both Judaism and Christianity allow no such right of departure. That is because one's presence in the covenantal community is not voluntary but involuntary. That is, one is a member of the covenanted community because of God's election of the community into which one is born. Most Jews are born into the community, hence their status is as innate as any natural endowment. Similarly, many Christians are involuntarily baptized as infants, hence they are for all intents and purposes born or "born again" (*gennēsthai anōthen* is the New Testament's term for it) into the church as much as Jews are born into the Jewish people.[24] As for those who convert into the covenanted community as proselytes (also, "born again," i.e., *ke-qatan she-nolad*—the Talmud's term for it), their willingness to convert is only the necessary but not the sufficient condition of their actual conversion from gentile to Jewish status.[25] That is, although no forced conversion is valid, the community acting in *loco Dei*, as it were, has the right to either accept or reject any candidate for conversion. Indeed, the community's voluntary exercise of that right to either accept or reject any candidate for conversion is analogous to God's right to choose whichever community God wants for the covenant and to situate at birth any person into whatever community God wants that person to be. Moreover, like God, who we assume has good reasons for choosing to do what he does, so the community in the person of its authorities should have good reasons for their choices, too, in accepting or rejecting anybody who presents

---

24. See John 3:7. Even though "a Christian is not born but made" (*Christianos non nascitur sed fiat*) by baptism, postnatal infant baptism is as involuntary for Christians baptized as infants as is their conception or birth as Jews for Jews. Of course, I recognize that some Christians do not practice infant baptism.

25. *Yevamot* 22a; 47a. See Novak, *Election of Israel*, 177–99.

himself or herself for conversion. Yet unlike God, whose reasons for what he chooses to do are often mysterious to us, human authorities acting with a divine warrant from the Torah should have reasons for their choices that are evident to both members and non-members of their community.

Although one's departure from the community is a legal impossibility (because either birth in or conversion into the community is indelible and irrevocable), theologically speaking, it is a political reality nonetheless. In other words, what is impossible *de jure* is quite real *de facto*. Indeed, Jewish tradition itself recognizes that political reality, teaching that the community is no longer responsible for those who have departed from it, especially those who have joined another faith community and have thereby apostatized. And this is so despite the fact that the tradition still affirms the possibility of their "return to the fold" (*teshuvah* in Hebrew, usually translated as "repentance"). That is, no matter how far any Jews have strayed from the life of the covenanted community, they have the right to return to the community with impunity, i.e., the community may not refuse them reentrance *de facto* into the community they have not ever left *de jure*. However, until that return is a fact, anyone who has departed from the life of the community, that person is for all intents and purposes no longer a member of the community.

When premodern Jewish communities had political authority over their members (including even police power), they often had the power to keep individuals in the community involuntarily, against their will. Moreover, this led to the type of authoritarianism that did not see any point in even attempting to persuade members of the community to remain in the community, let alone be proactive in the community, because there seemed to be no need to do so. But the experience of living in democratic states, where citizenship is voluntary and membership in what are legally private associations is voluntary all the more so, has greatly influenced even orthodox or traditional Jews, who are faithful to the tradition *in toto*. It has made them realize that the only way they can actively remain in the traditional community honestly and encourage others to do so, is to regularly search for reasons why any rational God-seeking person would want to actively remain in the community or even remain there at all. In the Jewish traditions, this is the ongoing process of discovering what are called "the reasons of the commandments" (*ta'amei ha-mitsvot* in Hebrew). Nevertheless, failure to discover such reasons for any specific commandment of the Torah does not justify nonobservance. In such cases, the commandment is to be observed nonetheless because it is God's *will*, even though God's *wisdom* (i.e., God's rationality) in this case may not be yet known. As the Talmud puts it: "When the Torah seems empty, the emptiness is yours."[26] For many, this can be a hard teaching. However, one's acquiescence to divine authority alone, although necessary at times, should only be temporary, i.e., one should always hope that the divine wisdom by which and for which any commandment was so commanded will eventually become evident to those now keeping the commandment regardless.

Unfortunately, though, too many leaders in orthodox Jewish communities today are still quite authoritarian. And even though they do not have their old, premodern power of overt coercion, they still exercise various forms of social coercion through emotional pressure. However, orthodox Jewish feminists, no doubt due to their experience of greater female inclusion in secular society, are now very forcibly challenging this authoritarianism, especially its perceived misogyny. They do this by finding sources and reasons in the tradition, many of which have been long dormant, that indicate how the tradition itself can develop without abandoning its fundamental, nonnegotiable mandates. And these feminists are doing this because of their experience in democratic societies, *in* which they participate, neither being *of* them nor apart *from* them. Authoritarian orthodox leaders opposing these feminists often suffer cognitive dissonance because of them, because these women (and their male supporters) belie the presumption that anybody questioning this kind of authoritarianism is ignorant of the tradition and/or impiously nonobservant of its practices. Yet the great majority of these feminists are both learned and pious.[27]

BIBLICAL PRECEDENT IN THE BOOK OF ESTHER

For this participatory public stance, there is biblical precedent. When it seemed inevitable that King Ahasuerus's innovative, secular state through the government of Prime Minister Haman would destroy the Jewish people, Mordecai told Queen Esther that "respite and deliverance will arise for the Jews from another place" (Esth 4:14). This "other place" (*maqom aher*) seems to be the only allusion to God in the otherwise secular book of Esther. Yet Mordecai did not become a sectarian/separatist after God did save his people from Haman's genocidal plan. In fact, "Mordecai the Jew ranked

26. *Peah* 1:1, 15b (cf. Deut 32:47).
27. See JOFA.org, the website of the Jewish Orthodox Feminist Alliance.

next to [*mishneh*] King Ahasuerus" (Esth 10:3), meaning that he became Prime Minister in Haman's stead. Immediately thereafter, the text says that Mordecai "was highly regarded by the Jews and accepted [*ve-ratsui*] by the multitude of his brethren, seeking good for his people and speaking peaceably [*ve-dover shalom*] to all his stock." That means Mordecai (and Esther) was no longer the assimilationist he had been in the past. Instead, while becoming the fullest participant in what seems to be the pre-modern secular state of Persia, he never again succumbed to the temptation of being *of* the state rather than just *in* it. Moreover, by "speaking peacefully to all his stock," it could be said that Mordecai was not reenacting the type of authoritarianism that characterized the rule of Haman, that he and his colleagues were exercising a maximum of persuasion and a minimum of coercion.

Like Mordecai, though, even when we are most *in the world*, our beginning and our end is always *of* that *other place*. We do not expect salvation to be found or to be invented anywhere *in* this world. Therefore, the task of waiting for that ultimate salvation to come is the task of our traditional communities; it is not the business of the secular state. The fruitful interaction of our traditional communities—Jewish, Christian, and Muslim—and the secular state requires constantly recognizing that the participation of each in the life of the other—a participation that is neither obsequious nor imperialist. That is what is truly best for both religious communities and the modern state.

2

Tradition
A Catholic Understanding

James L. Heft, SM
University of Southern California

In THE 1964 MUSICAL *Fiddler on the Roof*, in the song entitled "Tradition," the main character, Tevye, perched on a rooftop, describes tradition as keeping his balance and, without falling off and breaking his neck, fiddling a "simple tune." Tradition is important because, he tells us, it guides everything: "How to eat, how to sleep, even, how to wear clothes." When he asks himself how these traditions started, he admits, "I don't know." But even without knowing the origin of these traditions, he knows that they are important, because by following them, "everyone knows who he is and what God expects him to do."

Why does he describe tradition as a balancing act? Between what and what? It is a balancing act between what to keep and what to change. Tradition, as David Bentley Hart writes in his chapter, is necessarily an "ambiguous" reality: on the one hand, it has to keep what is fundamental to a religious tradition, while on the other, be willing to make changes without changing what is fundamental. A balance between these two characteristics

33

of tradition—fidelity to the core of the tradition while making necessary adjustments needed to live in changing times and cultures—characterize a living tradition. Tradition requires careful attention because all of its rich aspects are not known; they require discovery and development over time. Tevye doesn't know where his traditions come from, but he knows that they are important. He lacks historical knowledge of the their origins, but he knows their existential value. There is always more to a tradition, as we will see, than what can be known or articulated at any given time.

As our editor has mentioned, some authors distinguish tradition from traditionalism: tradition is the living faith of the dead, while traditionalism is the dead faith of the living.[1] Traditionalism refuses to change anything, but tradition requires some change so that the tradition may remain vibrant in new circumstances and when faced with new challenges. Besides tradition and traditionalism, there is a third form that tradition can take, one that is contemptuous of any normative character: it claims to be tradition-less, creating an empty space or a blank page on which anything can be written, where everything is presumed to be, to use a colloquialism, "up for grabs." This type of "tradition," quite contemporary in the Western world, undercuts all traditions. It takes little to be contemporary; all that is necessary is to inhale.

All the authors in this volume deal with that tension between what needs to be kept (the normative) and what can and should change (the adaptive). All recognize, at some level, that there are three ways to deal with changes: forbid them, embrace them all, or sort out what can be changed and what can't. Instead of being totally in the world or totally apart from it, David Novak put it well when he writes that we need to be "a participant-in rather than a part-of or apart-from" the surrounding secular culture. What is needed, then, is a balance, or as the title of a book by the French philosopher Gabriel Marcel, *Creative Fidelity*, argues, tradition requires both fidelity to core of a tradition and change in non-essentials.[2] What it means to be both faithful and creative, however, is not always clear and can remain unclear even for centuries.

My task in this chapter is to describe how tradition is understood in the Catholic Church. I will begin my reflections with a description of how the bishops at the Second Vatican Council (1962–1965) described tradition. This description is based mainly on the document, *Dei Verbum*, literally, on

1. Pelikan, *Vindication of Tradition*, 65.
2. Marcel, *Creative Fidelity*, originally published in French as *Du refus á l'invocation*.

the *Word of God*, one of Vatican II's four dogmatic constitutions. In that document, the bishops spoke of revelation as a single source, thus affirming that the teachings of the Church must be consistent with Scripture, even if not explicit in it. Obviously, that formulation requires continuity (consistency) and openness to change (room for what is not yet explicit). Second, I want to describe who has a say in how tradition is understood and how it can and should change. In this section, the *sensus fidelium*, the sense of the faith of all the faithful, becomes foundational, while theologians and finally bishops bear responsibility for the official articulation of the faith. Third, while the faith of the laity, the work of theologians, and their collaboration with the bishops is often a contentious process, the results of conversations among them are often fruitful, especially when the conversation is sustained, respectful, and takes place at a time when change may be necessary. Finally, recent developments within the Catholic Church suggest a positive way forward, one more open to a deeper understanding of the various roles that the laity, bishops, and theologians play in the articulation of tradition and, therefore, more promising for finding common ground with other Christian traditions. I approach these issues as a historian, a Catholic theologian, and as someone deeply committed to ecumenism and interreligious dialogue.

VATICAN II ON THE UNITY OF SCRIPTURE AND TRADITION

In the Western Church, the trauma of the Protestant Reformation forced the Catholic Church to respond to Martin Luther's challenge of *Sola scriptura*, namely, that Scripture was the final arbiter of Christian truth. Luther himself was no literalist; he did not believe that everything had to be explicit in Scripture to be normative. He did affirm, for example, the doctrine of the Trinity (three persons in one divine nature) and the practice of infant baptism, neither of which is explicit in Scripture. However, he put such an emphasis on the centrality of Scripture that finding ways to legitimize normative traditions not explicit in Scripture had to be addressed.

In response to Luther, Catholic bishops gathered at the Council of Trent (1545–1563) and devoted considerable energy to articulating their understanding of the foundation of faith and how it was to be passed on. At one point in their discussions, they considered but then rejected the idea that revelation was to be found "partly in written books, partly in unwritten tradition." They chose instead to state that the gospel constituted the source of truth and the authoritative guide to the moral life and was handed down "in the written books and unwritten traditions." Given the conflict between the reformers and the bishops, it is not surprising that since then until the Second Vatican Council, the "written books and unwritten traditions" were often understood to be two separate and parallel sources, Scripture on one track and Tradition on the other. The real issue, however, is how the two relate. The polemics of the Reformation also led the bishops to seek to protect revelation through precise conceptual formulation of doctrines, which, as we shall see, overestimate their precision.

Beginning in the twentieth century, more and more Catholic scholars began to study the Bible critically. After some stops and starts during the first half of the twentieth century, Pope Pius XII published *Divino afflante spiritu* in 1943, an encyclical that officially opened the way for Catholic scholars to study the Bible critically. The pope explained that the biblical authors used different literary forms that scholars needed to take into consideration if the texts were to be properly understood and interpreted. Protestant scholars had already been studying the Bible critically, and Catholic scholars began, even before Vatican II, to join them in their research. The bishops at Vatican II clarified in *Dei Verbum* that Scripture and tradition form one sacred transmission of the word of God. They wanted oral and written traditions to be understood as mutually intertwined. They refused to adopt the phrase "two sources of revelation." Instead, they spoke of a single source, which they called tradition. Rather than think of revelation primarily in terms of propositions, the bishops spoke of communicating the word of God in its entirety. The primary revelation, then, is the person of Jesus, and the secondary is what we try to say, always inadequately, about that person in propositions. Finally, in the process of articulating the faith, the bishops were directed to draw upon the *sensus fidelium*—that is, of the faith of the entire people of God. Instead of thinking of themselves as teachers and the laity as learners, the bishops at Vatican II now emphasized that all the faithful were required to discern the faith, though the bishops bore a special responsibility to discern with theologians the faith of all believers before attempting to articulate it. If Karl Barth described the role of the theologian as one who thinks with the Bible in one hand and the newspaper in the other, theologians in the Catholic Church locate themselves between the laity and the bishops, facilitating among these groups in the light of Scripture a conversation in which all three parties continue to learn.

Obviously, when the core of the Christian revelation is a singular divine-human person, Jesus, the ability to describe that encounter is limited. Understanding that the articulation of the truth and meaning of Jesus Christ is always limited, the door remains open to better articulation at another time and place. In her chapter, Sarah Hinlicky Wilson describes how cross-cultural missionary activity, the passage of time, and the need sometimes to repudiate false understanding of the tradition all open the door to new articulations of the core of the tradition. Sometimes, important parts of a tradition are lost, as in the case of the active role of the laity participating in celebration of the Mass, reinstated by Vatican II. Along these same lines, Professor Moosa writes about the passion and politics in the Muslim world today that make needed, thoughtful reinterpretations of some teachings.

These are not the only reasons why it is necessary at times to rethink the tradition. There is still another important reason, already alluded to, why changes in teachings might be necessary: the inescapable limitations of language, especially heightened in any effort to articulate things divine. An important and little known document, published in 1973 by the office in the Vatican responsible for safeguarding orthodox teaching, stated that the definition of doctrines, including dogmas, can be at one and the same time true and still in need of constant reformulation because of a fourfold historical conditioning due to (1) the limited state of human knowledge at the time of definition, (2) changeable conceptions and thought patterns that belong to a certain period of time, (3) the specific concerns that motivated the definition, and (4) the limited expressive power of the language used.[3] As Professor Hart states in his chapter, Christian dogmas are just a little less open to reformulation than the entire tradition, and they embody a hidden dimension even within their wording of the truth of revelation: "Coherent dogma does not reduce but instead greatly enlarges the area of mystery within a creedal tradition and ultimately multiplies the questions that faith cannot yet answer."

It was the understanding of history, especially of the early Church (the first six centuries), that brought John Henry Newman (1801–1890) to focus his attention on how Christian doctrine necessarily develops. Ever since his 1845 *Essay on the Development of Christian Doctrine*, Catholic bishops and theologians have paid attention to how core teachings develop, authentically, over time. The bishops of Vatican II made significant changes in the

---

3. "Sacra Congregatio Pro Doctrina Fidei," 402–4. See also Heft, *John XXII*, 211.

Church's official teaching—changes such as embracing religious freedom and ecumenism and rethinking the continuing validity God's covenant with the Jews—that have been lauded by many but still contested by some ever since. As a consequence, how official teaching evolves came to the fore at the Council and since in a dramatic way.

Biblical literalists clearly forbid development to what is explicit in Scripture. But for those who believe that there can be development in doctrine, it is necessary to prevent arbitrary changes. The bishops at Vatican II stated a limit when they declared that when interpreting Scripture, they were not superior to it but rather its servant. In the constitution on Scripture, *Dei Verbum*, they wrote that they are required to teach "only what has been handed on, listening to it devoutly, guarding it scrupulously, and explaining it faithfully by divine commission and with the help of the Holy Spirit; it draws from this one deposit of faith everything which it presents for belief as divinely revealed."[4] Whatever the bishops teach, then, must not violate the Word of God.

Moreover, Vatican II made it clearer that official Church teaching must embody and express not just what bishops believe but also the faith of the whole Church. At Vatican I (1869–1870), the bishops declared in their definition of papal infallibility (*Pastor aeternus*) that the infallibility of the pope is to be understood as that same "infallibility with which the divine Redeemer willed that his Church should be endowed for the defining of doctrine concerning faith and morals."[5] That is to say, the infallibility promised to the pope "when he defines" is first and fundamentally that of the whole Church. Hence ecclesial infallibility is key to all other forms of infallibility. This means, I believe, that the consensus of the Church, shaped by the Holy Spirit, is the rule of faith for the pope.

The bishops at Vatican I did not, of course, anticipate Vatican II's commitment to ecumenism. The great ecclesiologist Yves Congar quoted the words of Luther with approval in his reply to the papal apologist Sylvester Prierias: "I don't know what you mean when you call the Roman Church the rule of faith. I have always thought that the faith was the rule of the Roman Church and of every Church, as the Apostles say: 'Peace and mercy to all who follow this rule' (Gal 6:16)."[6] In 1870, at the height of the ultramontane defense of papal authority, most of the bishops were preoccupied

4. Flannery, *Vatican Council II*, 755–56.

5. Denzinger, *Enchiridion symbolorum*, 616.

6. Congar, "*Magisterium*, Theologians, and the Faithful," 552–53.

with defending the authority of the pope. Those bishops could hardly have imagined what, in less than 100 years, the bishops at Vatican II would affirm about the importance of dialogue, the role of the laity, and ecumenism. According to Vatican II, the Catholic Church recognizes that there are authentic forms of Christianity operating outside the Catholic Church. It is therefore imperative for Catholics today to rethink what it means to speak about the faith of the entire church. The Catholic church can no longer exclusively be equated with the *Roman* Catholic Church.

BISHOPS AND THEOLOGIANS: A BRIEF HISTORY

Since the Council of Jerusalem (Acts 15), church leaders have met to resolve doctrinal controversies. In the early church, some bishops were also great theologians. One needs only to mention names such as John Chrysostom, Gregory of Nazianzen, Ambrose, and Augustine to recall the episcopal theological creativity of the patristic period. From the sixth century on, the theological work of monks such as Anselm and Bernard of Clairvaux retained their rich combination of pastoral and doctrinal dimensions. Learned bishops and monks played key roles in articulating the faith.

With the establishment of universities in the twelfth and thirteenth centuries, however, a rigorously academic or scholastic theology began to overshadow the pastoral theology of the patristic period and early monastic movement. In the universities, highly technical questions were debated and explored, such as the authority of the newly translated works of Aristotle. Some scholars even wondered whether those works to a significant degree might in fact displace the authority of the Bible. Mistrust often arose among different schools of thought. This is exemplified in the major controversy between the theologian Peter Abelard and the monastic leader Bernard of Clairvaux—the former, an advocate for a more academic theology; the latter, for a more pastoral/devotional approach.[7]

During the medieval period, few theologians were bishops. Given the increasing strength of universities, theologians there began to exercise increasing influence in determining what was to be accepted as orthodox teaching. They became a *magisterium*, a teaching authority themselves, like the bishops. During the Protestant Reformation, theologians continued to exercise considerable influence. Luther in fact appealed strongly to his academic credentials to legitimize the validity of his criticisms of the Church.

7. On this theological clash of titans, see Otten, "Authority and Identity."

At the Council of Trent, theologians examined and debated contentious issues in the presence of the bishops. Only after listening to these presentations and debates did the bishops formulate their own conclusions.[8] The Reformation, however, profoundly affected the tone of Catholic theological work; in the Tridentine era, it became defensive, confessional, adversarial.

Two centuries later, the French Revolution (1789) pushed the Catholic Church into an even more defensive posture. It had to combat not only Protestantism but also the Enlightenment, which, as David Novak writes in his chapter, was even harder for the Catholic Church to accept than it was for the Jews. For the first time, Jews could become full citizens of the state, while the Catholic church was significantly stripped of the civil power it had exercised for centuries. Those Catholic theologians who attempted to address some of the issues raised by the Enlightenment (e.g., the recognition of the historical character of doctrine, religious freedom, the importance of experience, and the role of the *sensus fidelium*) in a sympathetic way regularly came under episcopal scrutiny. From the first half of the nineteenth century through the Second Vatican Council, popes and bishops were determined not just to monitor the work of theologians but to control it. In 1863, for example, Pius IX published what was called the "Munich Brief," in which he declared that bishops were not just to oversee the work of theologians but also to direct it.[9] According to the theologian Joseph Komonchak, "Under Gregory XVI and Pius IX, every significant attempt at an independent encounter between faith and reason, between religion and modern society, came under suspicion if not outright condemnation."[10] Monsignor George Talbot, who served as Papal Chamberlain to Pope Pius IX, described Blessed John Henry Newman in 1863 as "the most dangerous man in England."[11] The following year, Pius IX published his well-known *Syllabus of Errors*, a sweeping condemnation of modernity.

8. See O'Malley, "Lesson for Today?" O'Malley explains: "The bishops at Trent were typical of the Catholic episcopacy at the time. They had little formal training in theology, even though they otherwise might be well educated according to the standards of the day. If they had university degrees, those degrees tended to be in canon law. The theologians at Trent, however, came exclusively from universities or comparable institutions, and some were men of great distinction. They were not hand-chosen to promote a particular perspective but represented a random sampling of theological 'schools.' The bishops did well to hear them out before proceeding to their own deliberations" (O'Malley, "Lesson for Today?," 13). See also O'Malley, *Trent*, 84–85, 92, 108, 131, 145, 154, 189.

9. Komonchak, "Modernity." See also Howard, *Pope and the Professor*, 95–114.

10. Komonchak, "Modernity," 374.

11. Gilley, *Newman and His Age*, 348. Henry Edward Cardinal Manning, Archbishop

One of the most significant ways that popes began to direct theological reflection in the Church was through the publication of encyclicals. For most of the history of the Church, popes mainly published only their decisions on various matters, not teaching documents or encyclicals. Beginning in the eighteenth century, this changed. Benedict XIV (1740–58) and Pius VI (1775–99) published only one and two encyclicals respectively. Pius IX (1846–78), thirty-eight, and Leo XIII (1878–1903), seventy-five, an average of three encyclicals per year. Unfortunately, as John O'Malley writes, "Even before but especially after the definition of infallibility, what popes said in their encyclicals tended to assume an irreversible quality."[12] This trend has continued to the present day and presents special difficulties when popes, through their encyclicals, attempt to act unilaterally as theologians for the whole Church.[13]

Before the nineteenth century, the word *magisterium* (from the Latin for "teacher") applied, as indicated before, in different ways to the work of both theologians and bishops. Especially after the 1870 definition of papal infallibility, the word applied only to those who taught with public authority—namely, bishops. Theologians taught only as private persons, without official authority. Today, the word *magisterium* is used almost exclusively to describe the teaching authority of the hierarchy. These changes weakened the teaching authority of the theologians and practically ignored the role of the laity in the discernment of the faith.

During the late nineteenth and early twentieth century, Catholics suffered through what has come to be called the Modernist crisis: an intense period of struggle between the papacy and various theologians believed to have ceded too much ground to the temper of modern times, particularly to modern rationality, radical biblical criticism, science, and liberal democracy. Theologians were required in 1910 by Pope Pius X (1903–1914) to take an oath against "Modernism," a catch-all category described by the pope as "the heresy of heresies."[14] Long lingering after-effects of this crisis, extending even into the 1950s, inflicted suffering on prominent Catholic

---

of Westminster and leader of the English Roman Catholic Church from 1865 to 1892, also deeply distrusted Newman.

12. O'Malley, *What Happened at Vatican II?*, 55–56.

13. Shortly before being elected pope, Joseph Cardinal Ratzinger wrote: "The pope is not an absolute monarch, whose will is law, but completely the opposite: he must always seek to renounce his will and call the Church to obedience, but he himself must be the first to obey" (Ratzinger quoted in Queiruga, "*Magisterium* and Theology," 55).

14. On the Modernist Crisis, see Kerr, "Different World."

theologians such as Yves Congar, Henri de Lubac, and John Courtney Murray, all of whom at some point were silenced and forbidden to publish.

But in 1958 the cardinals elected a new pope, who took the name John XXIII (r. 1958–1963) and who, despite his advanced age, surprised the world when he called for an ecumenical council to renew the life of the Church. At that Council, bishops and theologians interacted more extensively and fruitfully than perhaps at any time in the history of the Church. Bishops invited theologians to the Council to serve as their *periti* or theological advisors. Congar, de Lubac, and Murray participated in the discussions that formulated some of the key documents of Vatican II. This council balanced Vatican I's emphasis on papal primacy and infallibility with a strong affirmation of collegiality among the bishops, along with the important role of the *sensus fidelium* of all the believers. And for their part, theologians began once again to pay closer attention to the experience of the faithful as well as to the work of Orthodox, Protestant, and Jewish scholars.

This close collaboration between theologians and bishops seemed to usher in a new age of learning from each other. In 1966 Pope Paul VI (r. 1963–1978) wrote:

> Without the help of theology, the *magisterium* could indeed safeguard and teach the faith, but it would experience great difficulty in acquiring that profound and full measure of knowledge which it needs to perform its task thoroughly, for it considers itself to be endowed not with the charism of revelation or inspiration, but only with that of the assistance of the Holy Spirit.[15]

In the years since the Council, the dynamic and positive relationship between bishops and theologians has suffered new strains and difficulties, with the work of many theologians once again coming under close episcopal scrutiny, especially under the pontificates of John Paul II and Benedict XVI.

TOWARD A HEALTHY INTERACTION AMONG LAITY, THEOLOGIANS, AND BISHOPS

What sort of interactions among the laity, theologians, and bishops will contribute to the cultivation of a living tradition within contemporary

15. Paul VI quoted in Dulles, "Freedom of Theology," 21.

Catholicism? How and to what extent should the experience of the laity be taken into account before any doctrinal decision is made? What happens when bishops overreach their authority, theologians misunderstand their role, and the laity are ignored in the discernment of the faith? John Henry Newman played a key role in thinking about such questions and his thought on these matters remains instructive. As a Catholic convert, he labored under the hostile suspicions of bishops and the Vatican. In the opinion of Ian Ker, his prominent biographer, Newman nonetheless went on to make a "great contribution towards a theology of the Church"[16] in the third edition of his "Lectures on the Prophetical Office of the Church." There Newman wrote about three "indivisible though diverse" offices in the Church—teaching, rule, and sacred ministry. The Church, he wrote, is at once

> a philosophy, a political power, and a religious rite: as a religion,
> it is Holy; as a philosophy, it is Apostolic; as a political power, it is
> imperial, that is, One and Catholic. As a religion, its special center
> of action is pastor and flock; as a philosophy, the Schools; as a rule,
> the Papacy and its Curia.[17]

The laity along with its pastors is, according to Newman, where the faith is lived out. In his study of the patristic period, "On Consulting the Faithful in Matters of Doctrine,"[18] he highlights the critically important contribution to orthodox teaching that the laity made during the Arian controversy. He grants to theology a "fundamental and regulating principle of the whole Church system," and adds that the Church is in its greatest danger when the schools of theology are weakened or no longer exist. On the other hand, theologians cannot always have their own way; they can be "too hard, too intellectual, too exact, to be always equitable, or to be always compassionate."[19] Ordinary Catholics by themselves lapse into superstition,

16. Ker, *John Henry Newman*, 701.

17. Ker, *John Henry Newman*, 703. Newman continues: "Truth is the guiding principle of theology and theological inquiries; devotion and edification, of worship, our emotional nature; of rule, command and coercion. Further, in man as he is, reasoning tends to rationalism; devotion to superstition and enthusiasm; and power to ambition and tyranny."

18. It was originally published in 1859 as an article in *The Rambler*, and again, with some additions, in 1871 as an appendix to the third edition of *The Arians of the Fourth Century*. See Newman, *On Consulting the Faithful*.

19. Ker, *Newman*, 704. Friedrich von Hügel (1852–1925), writing in 1918, during the anti-Modernist period in the Church, described himself as seeking to do "all that I can

just as the hierarchy, Newman continues, left to itself, inclines to power and coercive control. When both theologians and bishops are attentive to, if not simply endorsing, the thought and practice of the laity, the *sensus fidelium*, all three will relate in a dynamic way, even if perfect concord among them may not necessarily result.

The capacity of the laity to help influence the formulation of correct teaching continues, of course, in our own day. At the 1980 Synod of Bishops on the family, for example, Cardinal Basil Hume of England stressed the need to consult the laity, especially on matters of family and sexuality. He explained that the prophetic mission of husbands and wives is based on their experience as married people "and on an understanding of the sacrament of marriage of which they can speak with their own authority."[20] Both their experience and their understanding constitute "an authentic *fons theologiae* from which we, the pastors, and indeed the whole Church can draw." It is, the Cardinal continued, because married couples are the ministers of the sacrament and "alone have experienced the effects of the sacrament" that they have special authority in matters related to marriage. Hume's recommendation anticipated the survey conducted by Pope Francis in preparation for the 2014 and 2015 meetings of the Synod on the Family.

The sense of the faithful, as Newman has shown, will not necessarily support every current teaching of the hierarchy any more than the bishops gathered at Vatican II supported all of the official Church teachings in force up until then. Pope Francis recently remarked that a good Catholic must *sentire cum ecclesia*; that is, a good Catholic must *think* with the Church, which does not mean, he added, thinking only in lockstep with the bishops.

Newman's ecclesiology has continued to influence thinking about the Church.[21] In a 1981 essay in the journal *Concilium*, the late Fr. Avery Dulles stressed that all three offices in the Church—the laity, theologians, and bishops—need to be open and receptive to each other. Reflecting Newman's

---

to make the old Church as inhabitable intellectually as I can—not because the intellect is the most important thing in religion—it is not; but because the old Church already possesses in full the knowledge and the aids to spirituality, whilst, for various reasons which would fill a volume, it is much less strong as regards the needs, rights and duties of the mental life" (Von Hügel, *Letters to a Niece*, 141).

20. Hume, "Development of Marriage Teaching," 276.

21. Again, von Hügel, who acknowledged a great intellectual and spiritual indebtedness to Newman, distinguished three important, interacting dimensions in the life of the Church: the institutional, the intellectual, and the mystical. See Von Hügel, *Introduction and Biographies*, 50–82, esp. 61.

thought, Dulles explained that bishops, isolated from theologians and the laity, tend to "encourage passive conformity and blind conservatism." Then they are tempted to "suppress troublesome questions," and "avoid new and provocative issues such as, in our day, the changing patterns of family life and sexual mores."[22] During the first thirty years of his life as a Catholic, Newman suffered from overbearing episcopal authority. It became almost unbearable for Newman shortly after the Vatican's definition of papal infallibility when some bishops, including Britain's own Cardinal Henry Edward Manning, seemed content with almost limitless papal authority. Newman wrote, "We have come to a climax of tyranny. It is not good for a Pope [referring to Pius IX] to live 20 years. It is an anomaly and bears no good fruit; he becomes a god, has no one to contradict him, does not know facts, and does cruel things without meaning it."[23] (The pontificate of Pope Pius, from 1846 to 1878, was one of the longest pontificates in history.)

Not only does the hierarchy need to be checked. Theologians also need to be checked because of "their love of speculation" and their inclination "to neglect the spontaneous piety of the people and the practical wisdom of the pastoral leaders." They become "infatuated with their own systems and neglectful of the beliefs and practices that do not fit harmoniously into their own mental categories." In the light of Vatican II, Dulles also notes that in distinct but not separate ways, bishops and theologians both have the responsibility constantly to do their best to discern the faith of the Church, including especially the laity, who, day in and day out, live the Catholic faith in "the trenches." None of these three groups in the Church, concludes Dulles, should take over the specialization of the others and reduce them to "innocuous servitude."[24]

In the same 1981 volume of *Concilium*, Yves Congar contributed a summary essay in which he returned to the dangers described by Dulles. According to Congar, both bishops and theologians are accountable to Scripture, tradition, and the faith of the people. Everyone in the Church, including the bishops, is required to seek the truth. Congar argues that all theological research should focus not on infallibility, but on "'life in the truth of Christ' (1 Cor 12:3)."[25] He also writes that theologians, when in-

22. Dulles, "Successio Apostolorum," 64.

23. Newman, *Letters and Diaries*, 25:231.

24. Dulles, "Successio Apostolorum," 64.

25. Congar, "Towards a Catholic Synthesis," 69. "Infallibility—a terribly weighted term which we need to use very warily—is a function of truth. We must not make

terpreting documents issued by the bishops, need to go "beyond a naïve reading" of them and offer instead a "maturely critical understanding and a re-rendering that meets the needs of the educated world today."[26] Concerning the faith of the whole Church, the *Sensus fidelium*, he gives great importance to Christian practice, especially in situations of oppression, injustice, and—above all—in the witness of martyrs: "The blood of witnesses guarantees the seriousness involved."[27]

The philosopher Alasdair MacIntyre, as mentioned by our editor, famously described tradition as a socially embodied and historically extended argument.[28] It is not unusual, I think, that a philosopher would describe tradition as an argument carried on by scholars. However, the heart of the tradition is not found first in the intellectually precise formulations of doctrines wrought by scholars and bishops. In his study of the fourth century, Newman located the foundation of orthodoxy in the "faith of uneducated men." He quoted the church fathers, who said: "The ears of the common people are holier than are the hearts of the priests." Jaroslav Pelikan explains that for Newman, tradition was "a profoundly democratic concept, which did not trickle down from theologians, popes, and councils to the people, but filtered up from the faithful (who are the church) to become the subject matter for the speculations, controversies, and systems of the dogmatic theologians."[29]

All believers, then, beginning with "uneducated men," need to listen carefully if they are to discern the truth of the gospel. Hart emphasizes the importance of a "hermeneutical piety," an intellectual humility, a "tacit awareness" in the face of what is always beyond any neat conceptual formulation. Contrary to rationalistic ways of thinking, the philosopher of science Michael Polayni writes of the "tacit dimension," of how we can know more than we can tell, and how trust and openness are essential preconditions for insight into the possible meanings of scientific reality or, in our case, revelation.[30] Similarly, Christianity's apophatic tradition of the *via negativa*, the negative way of knowing, plays a similar role, emphasizing that what we

---

infallibility the foundation stone of our structures and make truth a function of it."

26. Congar, "Towards a Catholic Synthesis," 75.

27. See Heft, "'*Sensus fidelium*' and the Marian Dogmas."

28. See MacIntyre, *Three Rival Forms*.

29. Pelikan, *Vindication of Tradition*, 80.

30. Polanyi, *Tacit Dimension*. See also his major work, *Personal Knowledge*. Avery Dulles linked Polanyi's notion of "personal knowledge" with Newman's "illative sense."

don't understand about God is much greater than what we do understand. In the words of the sixteenth-century mystic and poet John of the Cross, Christians need to "learn to understand more by not understanding than by understanding."[31]

All three "offices" in the Church—laity, theologians, and bishops—are called to be obedient to the truth of the gospel. It makes sense, then, for bishops to remind not just the laity and, especially, theologians—as is the custom in most episcopal documents—but also themselves, to discern carefully the faith of the whole Church which "filters up" to them, to be temperate and cautious in their pronouncements, to avoid scandal in their words and deeds, and, above all, to search for and be obedient to the Truth as it is lived out by the faithful.

Newman, Dulles, and Congar stress the interaction and openness that should characterize the laity, theologians, and the hierarchy. They recognize these distinctive roles without pitting them against one another. All three theologians personally experienced how these three dimensions of the Church could be in tension with each other. But they also stress that such tensions should nevertheless be expected, even welcomed, for the sake of maintaining a living tradition.

NEWMAN'S PLEA FOR THEOLOGICAL ELBOW ROOM

During some periods in the life of the Church, those tensions—especially the ones that arise between theologians and bishops—are not welcomed. This was especially true in the aftermath of the French Revolution. Theologians were kept on a short leash during the nineteenth and the first half of the twentieth century. During that difficult time, arguably no religious thinker made more eloquent arguments for the necessary freedom of theologians than John Henry Newman. Newman never thought of himself as a theologian but more as a religious thinker, even a religious controversialist. Yet his books, articles, and letters, taken together, have benefitted the work of theologians immensely, describing how tensions between theologians and bishops can be best handled and how the faith of the entire Church ought to play a major, collaborative role in the discernment of what should count as its normative tradition.

31. John of the Cross quoted in Rolheiser, *Wrestling with God*, 99. Also of interest is Firestone et al., *Learned Ignorance*. In that volume, I contributed a chapter entitled "Humble Infallibility."

During the nineteenth century, bishops gave little support to theologians who tried to explore how the Church could best respond to the challenges of the Enlightenment. Aware of the length of time that Tridentine Catholicism held sway, historian John O'Malley described the period from the culmination of the French Revolution in 1789 to the death of Pope Pius XII in 1958 as the "long nineteenth century." Newman, who lived through much of that period, fought for greater freedom for theologians to do their work and did not hesitate to describe the inevitable tensions between theologians and bishops in a somewhat apocalyptic way as an "awful, never-dying duel."[32] Except for the work of theologians like Newman and the German scholars Ignaz von Döllinger and Johann Adam Möhler, theological creativity at this time was the exception, not the rule. In his private correspondence, Newman often complained about the overreach of the hierarchy. Explaining his reluctance to publish his own theological work, he wrote that

> as well might a bird fly without wings, as I write a book without the chance, the certainty of saying something or other (not, God forbid! Against the Faith), but against the views of a particular school in the Church, which is dominant. I cannot accept as of faith, what is not of faith; who can? I cannot, as I said before, work without elbow room. I cannot fight under the lash, as the Persian slaves. To be the slave of Christ and of His Vicar, is perfect freedom; to be the slave of man is as bad in the mind as in the body. Never, as I know, was it so with the Church, as it is now, that the acting authorities [at] Rome . . . have acted on the individual thinker without buffers. Mere error in theological opinion should be met with argument, not authority, at least by argument first.[33]

---

32. Newman, *Apologia pro Vita Sua*, 224. For an excellent study of another nineteenth-century theologian, Ignaz von Döllinger, see Howard, *Pope and the Professor*. Both Newman and Döllinger immersed themselves in the study of the history, Newman drawing on his study of the Patristic period and the idea of development, and Döllinger on the history of the Church that led him to oppose the definition of papal infallibility, as well as commit himself to serious ecumenical efforts.

33. Newman, *Letters and Diaries*, 21:48–49, quoted in Komonchak, "Catholic University in the Church," 46. Some authors have found fault with Newman for being hyper-sensitive, just as Erasmus, writing to his friend Thomas More, faulted theologians of his day as "a remarkably supercilious and touchy lot" (Lash, *Seeing in the Dark*, 19). Newman was indeed sensitive, but not supercilious. Now that he is one step away from being canonized as a saint in the Catholic Church, Newman's forthrightness should be an encouragement for all theologians.

The buffers to which Newman refers protect the ordinary give and take between theologians, free to write what they think and to criticize one another without the fear of immediate hierarchical intervention. Newman explained that the great theological vigor of the medieval schools depended on theologians who were allowed "free and fair play" and did not feel "the bit in their mouths at every word they spoke." Instead, he believed that spirited debate displaced weak arguments with stronger ones. Only when such disputes became dangerous for the whole Church did Newman think that hierarchical intervention was appropriate, as it was in the seventeenth and eighteenth centuries, for instance, when the Jesuits and Dominicans were ordered to stop arguing about grace. Newman lamented that the great theological schools of Europe were destroyed by the French Revolution. That theological vacuum, he complained, was filled by schools of one mindset in Rome.[34] There, the dominant school of theology, in its early formative stages, was manualist scholasticism, an uncreative attempt to imitate medieval scholasticism; it was averse to newer forms of historical inquiry and transmitted in dry seminary textbooks. In Rome, many assumed it to be the only orthodox form of theology. Newman worked out of a different tradition—one grounded in the writings of the fathers of the church, sensitive to historical development, and often inductive, aware of the psychological and pastoral dimensions of believing and living the faith. Representatives of scholastic manualism, who became even more dominant during the early twentieth century, were the very theologians who helped silence Congar, Murray, and de Lubac in the 1950s.

In 1990, after over five years of consultation with bishops and the leaders of Catholic higher education throughout the world, the Vatican published an important document on Catholic higher education, *Ex corde ecclesiae*—literally, "from the heart of the Church"—referring to how universities grew out of the Church's cathedral schools in the twelfth and thirteenth centuries. That document spells out the role of bishops in their relationship to Catholic universities better than Newman's Irish bishops did. *Ex corde* gives support to a real university and does not conflate its role with that of a seminary. It does not claim for bishops any direct role in the running of Catholic colleges and universities and grants to universities institutional autonomy and academic freedom, "properly" understood.[35]

34. Newman, *Letters and Diaries*, 20:447, quoted in Komonchak, "Catholic University in the Church," 46.

35. John Paul II, "On Catholic Universities."

Newman actually anticipated much of *Ex corde*. In some ways he went beyond it. As a Catholic, he criticized bishops who held theologians on a short leash. If theologians were to render a real service to their students and to the Church, Newman insisted they needed "elbow room." Obviously, Newman remains especially relevant in our own day when there is so much potential for polarization. An essential part of that necessary "elbow room" was the assurance of due process. When that is missing, bishops put theologians under strict supervision, and their creative theological work, necessary for a living tradition, suffers.

"SAUSAGE MAKING" IN REAL TIME

The Church, an institution with a divine mission, is also a very human institution. Those who have written about the day-to-day problems of its governance and the controversies that arise over efforts to articulate the faith in the midst of times of change often suggest that the uninitiated might best stay out of the engine room of the barque of Peter or be more edified by not knowing how the sausage of Church doctrine is made. Two fairly recent and enlightening descriptions of how leaders of the Church at the Second Vatican Council went about making sausage are historian John O'Malley's previously-mentioned book, *What Happened at Vatican II?* (2008), and Yves Congar's *My Journal of the Council* (2012). Together, these books raise an important question: how might the inevitable disagreements between theologians and bishops redound to the good of the Church?

As already noted, the changes brought about by Vatican II were at once unexpected and far-reaching. One might therefore assume that with such significant changes—its recognition of the central role of the laity, its support for dialogue with the Orthodox Churches, Protestants, and members of other religions, its declaration of religious freedom, and its recognition of the inescapable effects of history even on formulations of infallible teachings—that the dynamic balance the rooftop Fiddler achieved had arrived once again for the Church, that theologians and bishops would continue to enjoy a fruitful tension with each other, and that, together, they would pay even more attention to the faith of the laity. But alas, the messianic age of balance has not yet arrived! Newman observed that Church councils have "ever been times of great trial"[36] and that understanding them and implementing their decisions can take time, even a century or two. We should

36. Newman quoted in Ker, "Wisdom of the Future," 14.

not be surprised, then, that problems between theologians and bishops have continued to arise. According to some historians, Vatican II marked the first shift away from forms of highly centralized authority, which began with the Gregorian Reform in the eleventh century and intensified during the Reformation and French Revolution, when Christendom—a church with political power—had to confront withering anticlerical opposition.

We see a lack of balance and due process between theologians and bishops play out in the recent case of theologian Elizabeth Johnson and the US bishops. In Johnson's case, the bishops' doctrinal committee did not follow the due-process procedures outlined in the 1989 document, "Doctrinal Responsibilities: Approaches to Promoting Cooperation and Resolving Misunderstandings between Bishops and Theologians," written by theologians, canon lawyers, and bishops and approved by the National Conference of Catholic Bishops. Instead, the bishops' Committee on Doctrine decided to publish, without any prior conversation with Johnson, severe criticisms of her 2007 book, *Quest for the Living God: Mapping Frontiers in the Theology of God.*[37]

In response, the theological community strongly criticized the bishops' lack of any conversation with Johnson. In reply, the bishops explained that the 1989 document was intended for the use of an individual bishop dealing with an individual theologian in his diocese. Johnson's case, they claimed, transcended any one diocese, so widely read was her book. The doctrinal committee then issued a "pastoral resource" for bishops, explaining their responsibilities as official teachers of the faith.[38] In it, bishops are encouraged to maintain a close relationship with the theologians in their diocese. Once again, however, the appropriate juridical protection for theologians was missing. Without that juridical protection, the rights of theologians are overlooked—rights that, according to the 1989 agreement, include "the right to a good reputation, and, if needed, the defense of that right by

---

37. Johnson, *Quest for the Living God.* For the texts of Johnson's spirited and incisive response to the bishops, see Gaillardetz, *When the Magisterium Intervenes,* 213–73. For a more general treatment of how authority should work in the Catholic Church, see also Gaillardetz, *By What Authority?,* a revised and expanded version of his 2003 book by the same title. Finally, another reliable authority on these issues is Sullivan, *Magisterium.*

38. The text, as well as all the major statements regarding Johnson's book and her exchanges with the bishops' doctrinal committee, can be found in Gaillardetz, *When the Magisterium Intervenes.*

appropriate administrative or judicial processes within the Church," and "in cases of dispute the right to expect access to a fair process."[39]

A lack of due process on the part of bishops is not the only problem that increases tensions in our own day. Online channels of communication and social media outlets often misunderstand, promote, and even distort controversies in the Church. Digital media not only democratizes the voices within the tradition, it also contributes to the centralization and reach of episcopal and papal authority. It is now very easy to form like-minded enclaves and special-agenda organizations not limited geographically. Instead of sustaining "the complex orthodoxy and orthopraxis of a tradition," these groups gravitate around a single issue or a cluster of similar issues, creating a narrowly defined identity that empowers people in our diffuse society. There are very vocal groups of Catholics, for instance, focused on pro-life, on the one hand, or social justice, on the other.[40] These single issue-groups have little time or interest for careful analysis. Newman dealt only with newspapers and asked bishops for the time theologians needed to work out their differences before an episcopal intervention. In our age, digital and electronic media make immediate interventions on the local level more likely. Pope Francis has been criticized for exercising precisely that episcopal restraint that Newman wanted.

ENCOURAGING SIGNS

Despite these challenges, there are some positive developments within the Catholic Church today. In 2012, the Vatican's International Theological Commission (ITC) published "Theology Today: Perspectives, Principles, and Criteria." The ITC is comprised of an international group of theologians appointed by the Vatican to study issues and report their findings to the Congregation for the Doctrine of the Faith (CDF), the principal Vatican organ for maintaining correct teaching. Its latest study is good news for several reasons. It affirms that "years following the Second Vatican Council have been extremely productive for Catholic theology" (art. 1) and praises the development of multiple theologies, because revelation is "too great to be grasped by any one theology" (art. 5). It affirms the historicity of revelation (art. 22, 29) and the use of both historical-critical and theological

39. See USCCB, "Doctrinal Responsibilities" par. 8.

40. Tilley, "Culture Warriors," 9, 11. Tilley describes astutely how identity politics polarizes the Church in the US.

methods of interpretation (art. 22), argues that the Church's living tradition should never "fossilize" (art 26) and that theologians are called to be "constructively critical" of movements in the Church (art. 35), and acknowledges the importance of distinguishing different levels of teaching authority (art. 37). It underscores the critical importance of the *sensus fidelium* (esp. art. 33–36) and mentions lived spiritual experience as an important source for theology (art. 88–94). It explains that

> bishops and theologians have distinct callings, and must respect one another's particular competence, lest the *magisterium* reduces theology to a mere repetitive science or theologians presume to substitute [for] the teaching office of the Church's pastors. (art. 37)[41]

This acknowledgement of the creative role of theology suggests that bishops should not automatically suspect theologians who go beyond simply repeating the formulations of the *Catechism of the Catholic Church*.[42] However, as positive as the ITC's statement is, it rarely cites the work of any major modern theologian (e.g., Karl Rahner on the self-communicating mystery of God, Hans Urs von Balthasar on the beauty of revelation, or Bernard Lonergan on theology as a framework for creative collaboration), and makes no recommendations on how to protect theologians' rights and freedoms. Although the document states that all criticism is to be "constructive," there will surely be differences of opinion as to what constitutes "constructive" criticism. And while the unity of theology is understood as not requiring uniformity, the degree of legitimate diversity will continue to be contested. One of the greatest assets of the Catholic Church for sustaining and clarifying what it understands as normative tradition is centralized authority. One of the greatest challenges the Catholic Church faces today is how to exercise that centralized authority in ways that welcome the creative work of theologians and listen carefully to the *sensus fidelium*. It remains to be seen how much influence this ITC study will have on how bishops exercise their authority and discern the tradition with the laity. That this

---

41. See ITC, "Theology Today."

42. In a recent article in *US Catholic*, Heather Grennan Gary quotes from a letter by Cardinal Donald Wuerl, archbishop of Washington, DC, to his seminarians, in which he warns them that "there are theological writers who present teachings contradictory to that of the church's magisterium." He tells them that if they have doubts about whether something a theologian writes contradicts the teaching of the Church they need only consult the *Catechism of the Catholic Church*. See Gary, "What Women Theologians Have Done."

document exists and is approved by the Vatican, however, is a hopeful sign.[43]

Additionally, there are clear public recommendations by prominent and well-respected Catholic theologians today on how bishops might improve their relationship with theologians. Shortly before he died in 2008, Cardinal Dulles wrote that bishops should do more to moderate charges and counter-charges between theologians of different schools, avoid issuing too many statements that appear to carry with them an obligation of assent, consult with a wider variety of theologians before issuing any binding statement, anticipate objections and seek to address them before issuing a statement, and, finally, be more sensitive to multiple cultures in the world.[44] Gerald O'Collins, a long-time professor at the Pontifical Gregorian University, called for similar reforms. He stressed the importance of respecting subsidiarity (i.e., allowing matters to be addressed locally first, and if unable to be resolved at that level, only then in Rome—something that Pope Francis, too, has said repeatedly). O'Collins also recommended that a more diverse and internationally representative group of theologians advise the CDF and he especially emphasized that bishops should recognize "the right of the accused to be present from the outset, to meet their accusers, to be given the accusations in writing well beforehand, and to be represented by someone of their own choice"[45]—something that never happened in the Johnson case.

Finally, today we can be grateful that Pope Francis has emphasized the role of the *sensus fidelium*. Leading by example, he regularly consults the laity. For instance, he wanted to know what the laity thought about the issues that would be addressed at the Synod on the Family. He sent out a survey to all Catholics, asking their opinions on marriage and the family. He did the same in preparation for the Synod on Youth and Vocation, and invited about 300 young people to meet with him in March of 2018. While it is too soon to tell what difference this pope will make in how we understand the

---

43. In an article suggesting ways to improve the processes used by the CDF, Gerald O'Collins notes that "frequently the texts coming from the ITC and, especially, the PBC [Pontifical Biblical Commission] have handled their sources more skillfully, argued their case more compellingly, and, in short, produced more convincing documents than those coming from the CDF itself. Would the CDF enhance its standing by authorizing and publishing as its own the texts of the PBC and the ITC?" See O'Collins, "Art of the Possible," 7.

44. Dulles, "Freedom of Theology," 22–23.

45. O'Collins, "Art of the Possible," 6–7.

roles of the bishops and theologians and the importance of the faith of all the people of the Church, we can at least conclude that he has already made a difference in the way the Church's central authority is exercised.[46]

CONCLUSION

The relationship between bishops and theologians remains a critically important issue for the Catholic Church. There are many reasons to keep that relationship dynamic and positive. To be sure, much progress has been made on this matter since and because of Vatican II, but when the balance on the rooftop that Tevye sang about has been shaken, setbacks have also occurred. Especially at such moments, Christians should continue to exercise the virtue of hope and remain in respectful conversation with one another. David Bentley Hart reminds us that a living tradition is shaped by a hermeneutical practice, one that requires docility to and wisdom in the ways of the Holy Spirit, a "devotion to the limitless fecundity of the tradition's initiating moment or original principle, a certain trusting surrender to a future that cannot alter what has been but that might nevertheless alter one's understanding of the past both radically and irrevocably." As the theologian Nicholas Lash once wrote: "Optimism and despair already know the outcome—they prematurely complete the story."[47] Optimism and pessimism are implicitly totalitarian, he explains, whereas hope is open and confident, if not presumptuous, about the future. The foundation for hope should be found in the search among clergy, theologians, and laity for the guidance of the Holy Spirit, even as all parties stay in conversation with one another. In this way, a living tradition can be maintained and extended to future generations.

46. For an excellent recent study of the impact of Pope Francis on the shape of contemporary Catholicism, see Dillon, *Postsecular Catholicism*.

47. Lash, *Seeing in the Dark*, 15.

3

Tradition and Authority
A Vaguely Gnostic Meditation

David Bentley Hart
University of Notre Dame

ALONG THE UNEVEN COURSE of history's flow, there are those rare, odd turns in the streambed at which—due to a very special set of conditions and an entirely chance confluence of forces—an obviously bad idea can seem like an extremely good one, and before reason or good taste can intervene, it is adopted. As time passes, other unpredictable conditions conspire to preserve that initial mistake, until what began as a mishap of circumstance is transformed by the relentless alchemies of habit into a fixed element of our world, and even sometimes into an institution invested with an immemorial authority, commanding not only our respect but our allegiance as well. Thus a foolish fortuity becomes an indispensable truth, an ungainly anomaly a golden standard; accident is converted into essence, contingency into necessity; the fly and the amber are one. No doubt certain examples perhaps have already occurred: the designated hitter rule, the celibate priesthood . . . Holland . . . But we may not always appreciate how profound a challenge this sort of random metastasis of a momentary error into a revered tradition poses for many of our certainties regarding the meaning of

the past and the continuities of culture. It should trouble us gravely to consider how easily any practice, just by persisting long enough, can be woven
inextricably into the deepest fabric of shared memory and belief. It should,
at the very least, make us question how confident we are in our ability to
distinguish between genuinely enduring truths and mere tenacious con-
ventions, or between healthy developments and signs of decadence. More
fundamentally still, perhaps, it should make us wonder whether we can be
absolutely certain that there really is such a thing as a *religious* tradition at
all, in any meaningful and logically cogent sense, in the sense that rational
faith requires (that is, at once a source of irrefragable authority and a warrant for new interpretive discoveries), or instead, whether the command
that a religious tradition exercises over our minds has really been produced
by nothing more than the mounting force of historical inertia.

Of course, we have to assume that such fears are baseless. And naturally, our first line of defense against doubt on this score is the one we
draw between true tradition and mere "traditionalism"—between, that is,
the subtle discernment required by fidelity to the former (the scrupulous
historical exactitudes, rigorous metaphysical interrogations, and tireless
quest for spiritual wellsprings) and the brutish obduracy characteristic of
devotion to the latter (the pathetic fascination with the extraneous and the
arbitrary, the militant enthusiasm for the vulgar and the dainty alike, the
concern for form rather than substance, the fastidious dread of gnats but
indiscriminate tolerance of camels).[1] In most cases, telling the difference
seems effortless—as simple a thing as sorting out the living from the dead,
tender affections from morbid obsessions, young love from necrophilia.
Speaking merely for myself, for instance, I have become especially annoyed
in recent years by certain kinds of Roman Catholic "traditionalists" whose
numbers have been growing in this country over the past, say, decade and
a half. I find it seductively easy to satisfy myself that I can recognize the
precise juncture at which their loyalty to sacred truth degenerates all at
once into a perverted adherence to corrupt customs. And it causes me
scarcely an instant's hesitation to admit that my judgments in the matter are
prompted as much by personal taste as by sober analysis. More often than
not, after all, the "traditional" Catholicism for which these benighted souls
yearn is clearly not that of the ancient or mediaeval church (which was, after all, what the *ressourcement* movement and the *"nouvelle théologie"* were
seeking to recover); rather, it is that of the Baroque era, which I happen to

1. See Pelikan, *Vindication of Tradition*, 65.

regard as the most decadent and repellent period of Catholic culture, both intellectually and aesthetically (in all things, that is, save music). A good number of them, in fact, at least among that tribe's theological *cognoscenti*, look back fondly to what John O'Malley once called Catholicism's "long nineteenth century": that grim period when theological creativity had been all but extinguished in the Roman Church and the particularly incoherent and debased system of "manualist" or "two-tier" Thomism reigned triumphant.[2] To me this is rather on the order of cherishing a desperate nostalgia for a debilitating case of jaundice that one vaguely recalls from childhood. And yet, even when I have made all due allowances for my own biases and private predilections, my dismay at this sort of traditionalism remains undiminished. I still cannot help but sense that among my "traditionalist" Catholic acquaintances there are far too many who love ritual only when it is high and dry, many more who adore the stern guidance of an unyieldingly firm ecclesial hand, and an altogether unsettling number with an insatiable craving for taffeta, lace, and ermine—and yet next to none who seem much interested in Christian charity or, for that matter, in Christ. Almost all of them, in my experience, seem far too ready to mistake nostalgia for piety and intransigence for principle. And no sooner do I allow myself the thought that this may all be a very uncharitable misperception on my part than I receive some startling confirmation of my original prejudice. Some months ago, for example, in a moment of weakness, just as I was drawing precariously close to magnanimously excusing a student for citing Reginald Garrigou-Lagrange (1877–1964) to me sympathetically, a column appeared in the magazine *First Things* that pulled me back from the precipice by forcibly reminding me just how grotesque this idolatry of the ornamental can be. Admittedly, the quality of that journal has declined steeply since the days when my dog was regularly writing for it; but this particular article, it seems to me, was indicative of an extremely troubling spiritual pathology. Written by a young editor named Matthew Schmitz, it was principally a celebration, at the expense of Pope Francis, of the protagonist in the HBO television series *The Young Pope*, as well as a particularly mawkish reverie about the grandeur that was Rome in the days of unapologetic clericalism. The Young Pope of the series is, it seems, a high ritualist, a severe formalist, a believer in structure and order, a Catholic triumphalist who wants the Vatican to purchase back the papal tiara. Schmitz, it seems, pines for such a pope, even though—as he notes—the character he is

2. O'Malley, *What Happened at Vatican II?*, 53–92.

praising also happens to be an unbeliever. The program's great central irony, it turns out, is that its protagonist is a champion of the institutional church but is not actually a Christian. This, though, did nothing to diminish our author's giddy enthusiasm. What does belief matter, after all, so long as the pontiff celebrates mass *ad orientem* in his magic ruby slippers? Of the series as a whole, he writes: "Reveling in supposedly old-fashioned garments like the papal red shoes and wide-brimmed *saturno*, it shows how attractive an unapologetically traditional Catholicism can be."[3]

Not to me, I have to say. Quite the opposite, in fact. Then again, I never cared for Liberace's or Wayne Newton's wardrobes either (I even thought Carol Channing's a mite *de trop*). These days, of course—except in the occasional photograph of the arch-traditionalist Cardinal Leo Burke or on Bourbon Street during Mardi Gras—one scarcely ever sees anyone wrapped in the full pavonine panoply of Baroque ecclesial drag (shimmering satin *mozzetta*, billowing silk *ferraiolo*, gauzy gossamer *rochet*, gleaming *zucchetto*, pavilioning *saturno*, or gaily tasseled *galero* . . .). But, on those rare occasions when I do catch a glimpse of some prelate of any rank swathed in the sumptuous clericals of bygone epochs, I have to confess that in the very next moment, my mind conceives an image of him being hurled down a very long flight of granite stairs, violently striking every step along the descent, until he comes to rest at last on the rough paving stones of the plaza below, an incarnadined shard of broken and moaning flotsam amid a sea of exquisite fabrics. I find it a soothing image. If I then allow myself to dilate upon the fantasy a little, four or five pale youths with lank hair, clad in leather jackets and pointed Spanish boots, approach, exchange wicked smiles, toss away their cigarettes, and begin kicking him in the ribs, groin, and coccyx; when they tire of this, they strip him of his prettiest accoutrements and run away laughing to a nearby pawnshop whose most regular clientele are the "exotic" dancers from the adult cabaret next door. Soon thereafter the hyenas arrive . . .

Oh, but I ought not wallow in this gorgeous idyll. I risk becoming malicious. Suffice it to say that I agree with Pope Francis that clericalism is a cancer in the body of any church. I believe that the days when Catholic priests dressed like petty royalty and demanded deference from the laity were among the darkest of Catholic culture. I laud Francis's jovially

---

3. Schmitz, "Waiting for a Young Pope." Yes, I recognize that there are examples of pathetic nostalgia for the past in my own Orthodox tradition; happily, none of them involves satin.

paternal mockery of young priests who like to preen about in the epicene frills and flounces and gewgaws of those times. I rejoiced, after his election, when he refused to have that ghastly matronly *mozzetta* draped over his shoulders. Not that I object to distinctive clerical garb, so long as it is properly shabby—worn cuffs, frayed collars, shoes mended with duct tape—but priests are servants to servants, slaves of slaves. They are God's janitorial service. They should dress as such. My own taste in clericals tends toward the austere black cassocks of the Eastern churches (which reserve more resplendent habiliments for liturgical uses alone). Rather than the Young Pope and his seventeenth-century sensibilities, my ideal would be Pope Celestine, who in AD 428 brusquely reproached bishops in Gaul for their elaborate finery: "We should be distinguished from common folk and others by our studiousness, not our attire; by our conduct, not our clothes; by purity of mind, not the care we lavish on our persons."[4] And it usually seems clear to me, this is not *merely* a matter of taste. It seems obvious, broadly considered, why one should think Celestine a more faithful representative of a truly Christian understanding of ecclesial office than, say, a modern American cardinal in Wisconsin who squanders a small fortune in diocesan funds on a ludicrous silk *cappa magna*, who luxuriates in exorbitantly opulent clerical garb, and who casually re-crucifies Christ every time he slips his soft, sleek, suety little fingers into his velvet gloves. "What did you go out into the wilderness to gaze at? A reed being shaken by the wind? What rather did you go out to see? A man clothed in soft garments? Look: Those wearing splendid garments and living in luxury are in the houses of kings" (Luke 7:24–26; cf. Matt 11:7–9); "He has pulled dynasts down from thrones and exalted the humble, he has filled the hungry with good things and sent the rich away empty" (Luke 1:52–53); "You lived on the earth in dainty luxury and self-indulgence. You have gorged your hearts on a day of slaughter" (Jas 5:5). It seems somehow important, at any rate, that the only splendid garments Christ ever wore were those cast about him by the soldiers of Herod before they returned him to Pilate (Luke 23:11), and the nearest thing to the regalia of high office a soldier's scarlet cloak, a reed scepter, and a crown of thorns. It hardly constitutes a violent leap of logic to conclude that it was Celestine who was the true disciple of the Man of Sorrows, inheriting and faithfully passing on a purer vision of the Christian life, while the aforementioned American cardinal is at most heir

4. "Discernendi a plebe vel caeteris sumus doctrina, non veste; conversatione, non habitu; mentis puritate, non cultu" (Celestine I, "Epistola 4").

to a particularly obnoxious species of clerical pomp and to a meretricious sartorial fashion that in a pestilential season attached itself to the tradition like a toxic parasite.

And yet the issue is rarely quite that simple.

AN EQUIVOCAL CONCEPT

To begin with, the very concept of "tradition" is incorrigibly equivocal. At least, it entails a certain necessary ambiguity regarding what kind of continuity it is meant to describe: in one sense, what is at issue is the continuity of unalterable practices and immutable beliefs, as preserved by the community to which they give shape; in another sense, however, it is the continuity of a dynamic process, one that accommodates ceaseless alteration without taking leave of the original impulse or truth that this process supposedly enucleates over time. And both senses are indispensable if the concept is to serve any very useful purpose at all: the word *tradition* must, that is, serve simultaneously as a justification for the retention of elements for which no intrinsic rationale can be adduced—or any rationale at all other than past practice—and also as a justification for the undeniable variety of historical configurations assumed and abandoned by what is supposedly a single enduring community or institution across generations. Any tradition that cannot be justified in both ways at once, at any given moment, is almost certainly one that is moribund. But this also means that the term *tradition* can very easily become a mystification of either stagnation or caprice (or, for that matter, of both at once): the former it can endow with the false grandeur of an ancient wisdom delivered once and for all, the latter with the modish allure of "doctrinal development." Of course, different faiths will tend to emphasize one side of the concept more than the other, as will different factions within each faith; some will be more jealous of the old forms, some more eager for the new. But in every case, the same question hangs suspended above all talk of tradition: whether there can possibly be any account of that tradition capable of holding what is unalterable and what ceaselessly changes together in a single consistent and plausible unity, or whether instead we speak of "tradition" simply in order to distract ourselves from the fundamental arbitrariness of our beliefs.

The kind of distinction drawn above, moreover, between true tradition and decadent traditionalisms, presumes that a tradition is capable of some kind of internal "originalist" critique of the forms through which it passes in the course of its history. But this presents something of a problem inasmuch as the very concept of a living tradition entails a kind of double (or even circular) logic. In one sense, every tradition draws its authority from some sort of initiating moment of awakening, revelation, or discovery (the call of Abraham, the Law at Sinai, the hearing of the Vedas, Easter, the Buddha's enlightenment, Lao-Tzu's oracles, the delivery of the Qur'an, Guru Nanak's awakening, and so on); and yet, no less essentially, the authority of that initial moment is validated only in and by the richness, capaciousness, and perdurability of the historical developments to which it can continually give rise (whether we attribute those developments to the working of the Holy Spirit or the wisdom of the ancestors or whatever else). Thus, to attempt to reduce the essence of a tradition to only a few simple, indispensable, inaugural principles, and so consign all the rest to the realm of the fortuitous or adiaphoral, is to forsake the idea of living tradition altogether and, in that very way, to also reduce the original source of the tradition to a punctiliar historical accident without any actual meaning or power. It can have no real consequences in time. Nothing then remains. A truly living tradition, therefore, must be capable of accommodating far more than what a strictly reductive originalism demands of its founding event, because these two poles—a tradition's original moment and its subsequent historical unfolding—legitimate one another reciprocally and inseparably. And the moment this principle is admitted, the critical solvency of the originalist position begins to wane away. This is not a trivial matter. The examples I have given so far are positively garish in their obviousness. Only a tragically diseased sensibility could find the monstrous spectacle of a *cappa magna* morally or aesthetically palatable. Anyone who can look at a cardinal wearing a *galero* and not immediately think of a drunkard wearing an exceptionally hideous lampshade is simply a hopeless philistine. Most cases, though, demand a far keener power of discernment. And over *all* cases there looms the shadow of an ominous dilemma: *either* there is no real distinction between the essential and the inessential in a tradition, which would entail that the tradition as a whole is devoid of any coherent rationale, meaning, or critical power; *or* the distinction between essential and inessential is immediately obvious, which would entail that the larger tradition as a whole is mostly dispensable, being little more than a chance coalescence of insignificant accidents wrapped haphazardly around what would otherwise be just an evident truth. Certainly the witness of history does little to help us discriminate between the thing-in-itself and its epiphenomena. There is not only far too much accumulation and retention but also far too much attrition and forgetting. Over time, practices and forms continually attach themselves only to fall away again unexpectedly, or else they persist for no discernible reason; the seemingly fixed proves transient, the seemingly ephemeral permanent, and no privileged vantage can be found from which one can tell the dancer from the dance. This is why it is, perhaps, that the authority of "tradition" can be invoked simultaneously in support of the most pitilessly reductive rigorism and also as a justification for an almost infinite plasticity of practice and expression (even to the point of explaining away seeming internal contradictions of principle or logic). And so, again, one has to ask whether the very concept of "tradition" is a cogent one or is instead essentially fanciful: a euphemism for whatever happens to happen, a mystification of sheer unguided eventuality; one damned thing after another; local memory or (as is more often the case) false memory, translated into habit and then preserved as irrational prejudice or sickly nostalgia.

If this is not the case, however, then it seems to me that whatever it is that is most vital to a tradition—whatever force or substance sustains it as a continuity amid incessant change—must also be that which is most inconspicuous, even invisible. If nothing else, if the source of a tradition's continuity were not in some sense essentially hidden, it could never pass through, provoke, or survive so many successive conceptual and practical configurations; if it were not something that silently abides amid change, the constantly inexpressible within each transitory expression, it could neither tantalize the new into existence nor banish the old to oblivion. How one knows this invisibility, however, is difficult to describe. What is known is not a phenomenon within religious experience so much as the intentional horizon within which any religious phenomenon is able to appear, as at once a comprehensible form and an inadequate symbol of a fullness of truth that has no final finite expression. It is the nimbus of the unseen that shines all around the seen, a boundless surfeit of meaning that lies beyond the scope of every formulation of the faith, an infinite distance that at once frustrates and continuously urges devotion and reflection toward a final rest. In a larger and perhaps ultimate sense, it is the horizon of a truly transcendental object of desire, the divine fullness that in its infinite simplicity is hospitable to limitless expressions but reducible to none. Faith itself, moreover, positively requires this hiddenness to live; the venture of fidelity is nothing other than a trust in the reality of some living truth that transcends the forms it animates. Otherwise, every historical transition would constitute a defeat. So, the believer who abandons faith's preoccupation with the invisible and instead adopts the traditionalist's desperate adherence to the beguiling contingencies peculiar to some particular epoch or school has effectively forsaken tradition altogether and sought refuge in sheer wistfulness. It is its perennially hidden truth that endows any tradition with whatever internal power of critical discrimination it may possess; only that always more urgent yet always invisible impulse can free the faithful mind from the appeal of mere transient historical attachments and inspire it, however mysteriously, to correct aberrations and deformities within the tradition. Admittedly, faith's knowledge of that hiddenness is at most a kind of unspoken awareness of something that can never be exhaustively translated into simple concepts or words; it is, at best, what John Henry Newman called an "illative sense."[5] Still, the proof that any tradition is a living one is precisely that it does not fiercely cling to every aspect of what it has inherited but instead exhibits an often astonishing ruthlessness in shedding the past, out of obedience to some still more original spiritual imperative. One might almost describe this as devotion to a secret history: so secret, in fact, that it can enter experience only indirectly, almost like a Lockean substance, wholly veiled by—and yet revealed only in—its accidents.

As for how we can know that this secret history is truly there to be told, when so much of the concrete history of a tradition consists in an unremitting sequence of accretions and dissolutions, we must in some sense rely on the evidence of that very process: its persistence, its obstinacy, its inexhaustibility. Still, obviously, every tradition must employ a set of hermeneutical tools to impose some kind of stability upon itself, and the nature of these tools varies radically from tradition to tradition. In the main, Christianity has placed enormous trust in the power of doctrinal definitions to elucidate its intrinsic rationality and to impose order upon its diverse expressions. But even these definitions—as the whole history of Christian theological factions and ecclesial confessions demonstrates—are invariably only a little less fluid in their acceptation than is the tradition as a whole in its cultural configurations. Certainly, dogmas bring nothing to a simple conclusion, in part because they themselves rest their claims to validity upon that still hidden surfeit of truth prompting them, which always promises infinitely more than any specific proposition can ever express and therefore maintains its hiddenness even within its official expositions. Everything is proximate at best, suggestive at most. The history of

5. Newman, *Essay in Aid*, 266.

doctrine tells us that every defined dogma is simultaneously a *terminus ad quem* and a *terminus a quo*, and can be neither without also being the other; if this were not so, the very historical situatedness of any doctrine would render it incredible. Each dogma is a concrescence and summary of any number of prior forces but also the inauguration of an entirely new series of interpretive departures, elaborations, questions, conflicts, quandaries, and resolutions. It is anything but some pure distillate of belief, extracting the tradition's essence from its larger medium and concentrating it in a fixed form. Coherent dogma does not reduce but instead greatly enlarges the area of mystery within a creedal tradition, and ultimately, it multiplies the questions that faith cannot yet answer. Simply put, dogmas establish certain boundaries but also invariably open up entire new vistas. And, again, they are credible precisely as consonant with that hiddenness that remains inexhaustibly more original (emanating from an irrecoverable initial moment in the past) and inexhaustibly more final (summoning us to a future in which at last we shall see no longer in a glass, darkly, but rather face to face).

THE USES AND DISADVANTAGES OF DOCTRINES

We should pause, perhaps, to note that the very concept of doctrinal *definition* is also an invincibly ambiguous one. The history of dogma, dispassionately surveyed, is not the chronicle of a seamless process of long-held beliefs crystallizing from more inchoate into ever more precise formulations, as if the development of doctrine were little more than the process of the church finding the right words to express convictions present in the community of faith from the beginning. If we look back with unprejudiced eyes to, say, the ecumenical councils of the Christian past and the dogmatic promulgations they produced, we discover nothing like the continuous preservation of some settled *consensus fidelium* against the perverse novelties of heretical factions, much less an inexorable evolution of received religious truths toward increasingly exact creedal epitomes. What we find instead is the fitful generation of often willfully vague formulae describing genuinely unprecedented models of Christian confession. While every dogma draws upon the practices and language of the past, it also constitutes at once a synthesis and an innovation, and may even so radically alter the meaning of past beliefs and claims that something entirely new is introduced into the tradition (albeit under the aspect of a *venerable* truth). This is inevitable. Dogmas arise when seemingly intrinsic contradictions appear within the evolution of a given tradition. And the conflicts produced by these internal stresses can, as a rule, be resolved only by the creation of new ways of not only expressing but also understanding the past; and only in this way can the tradition get past what would otherwise be insurmountable *impasses.* Then, no less inevitably, in each case a certain degree of willful historical forgetfulness must be cultivated so that a new version of the past can be invented, one purged of the very complexities and confusions that had demanded a new dogmatic definition in the first place. Where the essence of doctrine is concerned, it is often not enough to provide a satisfactory answer; it is necessary then to take the additional step of forgetting the question. What we call "orthodoxy" and "heresy" are retrospective and (to be honest) transparently ideological constructions—which is to say, *reconstructions* of what has been—meant to fortify every new doctrinal resolution by enfolding it in the misty mythology of some pure and exhaustive deposit of the faith wherein all later orthodoxies are always already present, like latent algorithms. Christians, of course, find it convenient to invoke the Holy Spirit's guidance whenever it becomes necessary to dispel doubts regarding the actual material history of doctrine—which, frankly, apart from this article of faith looks like little more than a unremitting succession of political compromises and rhetorical evasions. And nowhere is the principle of inspired tradition more fully and more audaciously advanced than in Newman's splendid speculative fantasia, *Essay on the Development of Christian Doctrine.* Even so, it is best to be honest here. Gore Vidal once remarked that everything changes except the avant-garde—and this is true: the attempt at originality for originality's sake tends with almost perfect regularity to eventuate in the trite and tediously predictable. But it is no less true that, as often as not, there is nothing so truly new as our "ancient" traditions. Just as the most "novel" ideas we venture are frequently mere recapitulations of old ideas, which have been largely forgotten precisely because they proved fruitless, so also the "timeless" verities we affirm are often wholly original and synthetic products of the special pressures of the present moment.

I do not mean to suggest, incidentally, that doctrinal definitions are not in any sense genuine developments of previous expressions of faith or that they are just fanciful superimpositions upon a history from which they do not naturally emerge. I simply want to make clear that they are as much feats of creative reinterpretation and invention as they are deductions inexorably derived from the evidences of the past. Whatever they preserve, they also revise. Hence the rather provisional shape of most dogmatic definitions, the minimalism and rather abstract formality of their phrasing. The conceptual contents of defined doctrines, when subjected to real scrutiny, invariably prove far more protean, mercurial, and elusive than the seemingly hard propositional form of those doctrines would seem to suggest. In the end, the principal effect of a dogma is to close down a few unprofitable avenues of theological questioning precisely by opening up countless new, potentially more expansive avenues. And each doctrinal determination necessarily calls forth a ceaseless labor of interpretation and reinterpretation; but for this labor, that dogma would quickly become opaque, empty, and dead. One need merely consult the historical record to confirm this. Theological traditions remain vital only insofar as they are, in any age, in the process of being reconstructed. This means that every established doctrine requires restatement in formulations that preserve the received teaching precisely by subtly but continuously refashioning how it is to be understood. And these formulations must be feats of recollection, of critical imagination, and of inspired invention all at once—principled constructions poetically shaped in the present, from the testimony of the past, in the light of an indeterminate future. No tradition could long survive if it were really only the cumulative consequence of the cultural and intellectual forces of its own past; to continue to thrive and advance, it requires formal and final causes as much as material and efficient, shaping and summoning it toward a *telos* beyond the configurations it possesses at any given moment.

Take, for instance, the first and most significant—at least, as the grand governing paradigm for all that followed in dogmatic history—doctrinal definitions of Christian tradition: those of the first two councils, Nicaea and Constantinople. The "Arian controversy" constitutes, for all Christian memory, that crucial moment when the institutional orthodoxy of the politically enfranchised and publicly supported church for the first time (for want of a better word) *legislated* the proper form for faithful confession, and in so doing demoted all seemingly incompatible forms of confession (however devout and intellectually sincere) to damnable expressions of faithlessness. Whenever Christians recite the Nicene-Constantinopolitan Symbol, and especially when they confess (in whichever translation they use) that the eternal divine Son is "*homoousios*" with God the Father, they are putatively reciting a digest of the faith that has been recognized "everywhere, at all times, and by all peoples" as the one true orthodoxy. Moreover, it has been the fate of Arius to be remembered not merely as *a* heretic but *the* heretic, the very archetype of all heretics—the man who, out of sheer perversity or malice, supposedly broke from the common belief of all good baptized Christians in what was still the faith's golden dawn, the wanton innovator who defied the word of Scripture and the teachings of the apostles by rejecting what the church had always unequivocally taught regarding the Son's full Godhead and coequality of the Father. All of this is, of course, utter nonsense. In Arius's own time, it would have been absurd to regard him as either a traditionalist or a rebel (in part, because the testimony of neither Scripture nor tradition was nowhere near so clear and homogeneous as later Christians were taught to believe). In point of fact, he was a profoundly conservative theologian and, in the context of Alexandrian theology, was without question a much more faithful representative of the oldest and most respectable school of Trinitarian speculation than were the partisans of the eventual Nicene settlement. Admittedly, his appears to have been an especially austere and unimaginative expression of the tradition in which he had been formed; but that is rather the point: if his teachings have been accurately reported (which cannot be assumed), it would seem that it was precisely because he was such a fierce traditionalist that he was unable to grasp the demands of tradition. Still, one can understand what motivated him. He was attempting to preserve a long established and extremely plausible "subordinationist" metaphysics, one that seemed successfully to unite the divine and created realms in a continuous hierarchy of powers while still nevertheless affirming the absolute transcendence of God the Father. He even, as far as he was concerned, had Scripture on his side. Even the first verse of John's Gospel seemed to honor the traditional distinction between God Most High—God as identified in Greek by the definite article: "*the* God," "*ho theos*"—and "God" (or "god") in a secondary, subordinate, and perhaps only honorific sense—"*theos*" sans article.

In much of the Eastern intellectual world of the empire during the first three centuries, in fact, and in Alexandria especially, something like a subordinationist metaphysics had long been the common property of pagans, Jews, and Christians. It was generally assumed that the highest divine principle, in its full transcendence, never came into direct contact with the world of finite and mutable things but rather, since the beginning, has expressed itself in some economically "reduced" form through which it created and governed the world. There had long been Platonists, like Plotinus and Porphyry, who believed that the transcendent One was mediated to the lower world only through an order of progressively more derivative divine principles. There had been Jewish thinkers, such as Philo, who believed that God was mediated to his creation by a viceroy or "Son" or "Logos," a "secondary divinity" who had been the subject of all the divine theophanies of Hebrew Scripture. Many Christians had always shared this view too. All parties to this vision had, with varying degrees of complexity or mythic richness, imagined the interval between God (or the One, or what have you) and this world to be populated by a hierarchy of greater and lesser powers. And all parties had also shared the conviction that the second "moment" of reality—the *Logos* or *nous* that most immediately proceeds from the supreme principle of all things—was a kind of economic limitation of its source, one that through itself directly, or through some yet more subordinate principle, constituted a kind of deferred contact between the highest divinity and the realm of discrete beings. And thus the whole of reality—terrestrial, celestial, and even divine—subsisted in a single continuum. It was a deeply attractive picture of things, and in its Christian version, seemed to make complete sense of the language of Scripture. And the theology of Arius was a perfectly plausible, if stark, specimen of this metaphysics. For him, it was simply the purest Christian piety to insist that the Father was utterly hidden from and inaccessible to all beings, even the heavenly powers, and that it was only through his Logos that anything was known about him. Even the claim that the divine Son was in fact a creature, who at one time had not existed, was not an especially exotic supposition. That same piety dictated that only the Father could be understood as "unoriginate" in any meaningful sense. Many Christian thinkers of the second century, certainly, had believed that the Logos had been generated only a little while before the making of the world, so that he could effect the work of creation. Moreover, many Christians had long identified the Logos with the greatest angel of the celestial court, the Angel of Mighty Counsel, a kind of heavenly high priest who served the inaccessible Father and who was his representative to all other beings, both there above and here below. As a traditional Alexandrian believer, then, Arius was clearly operating within the ambit of the faith as he had received it from a long Christian past. And frankly, it is little more than a ridiculous accident of history that his rather ordinary theological career should have become the occasion for resolving a crisis. The crisis, after all, was not one of creed and confession, since Christianity had long accommodated a vast variety of beliefs regarding the nature of the divine Son. Rather, it was a crisis of imperial policy: the new

Augustus, having adopted the faith, required a single visible structure of power and a single audible voice of doctrinal authority if the newly enfranchised institution of the church was to serve his ends and prove docile to his will. Arius was the victim in part of his own lack of imagination, but in larger part of the new political circumstances of his age.

This is why it is that the settlement of Nicaea did not bring the controversy to an end, incidentally. There remained a great many very faithful Christians out there who thought the Nicene formula, especially that daring and difficult word *homoousios*, had obscured a vital scriptural distinction—or, at least, a vital mystery that Scripture had left open. And so, in the long aftermath of the council, any number of theologians proposed alternative solutions that they thought might restore a sense of that distinction. Among those who rejected the Nicene formula, as we all know, there were the "homoeans" who preferred to describe the Son as being "of similar substance (*homoiousios*)" with the Father, and there were the "anomoeans" who regarded the Son as being altogether "unlike" the Father; but what they shared in common was their fidelity to a Trinitarian language that they correctly regarded as being far more ancient than that of Nicaea and plausibly judged to be more faithful to Scripture. That the imperial church spent the better part of a century agonizing over the difference between words like *homoousios* and *homoiousios*—a difference on paper, after all, of only a single letter—has frequently been an object of mirth and caricatured as a silly contest between indistinguishable abstractions. But, for the Christians of the fourth century, the entire intelligibility of their faith was at stake. There were many issues, of course, informing the debate—Scripture, liturgy, the common understanding of the faithful—but chief among them was the nature of salvation.

This was the crux of the matter, after all. It was an age in which salvation was still understood not, say, as some kind of forensic justification of the sinner before God followed by admission into a happy hereafter but rather as the real union of creatures with God himself. All parties to the doctrinal disputes of the time were committed to the belief that Christ had assumed human nature so as to free it from bondage to death and make it capable of a direct indwelling of the divine presence. For Athanasius or the Cappadocian fathers, for instance, the paramount question was how such union with the transcendent God was possible for finite creatures. If (to use the familiar formula) "God became man that man might become God," could it possibly be the case that the Son or the Spirit was a lesser expression of God or, even worse, merely a creature? Only God is capable of joining creatures to God; any inferior intermediary, especially one like the created Logos of Arius, will always be infinitely remote from God himself. The Cappadocian arguments against the Eunomians were numerous, complex, and subtle; but at their heart lay a single simple intuition: If it is the Son who joins us to the Father and only God can join us to God, then the Son is God in a wholly consubstantial sense; and if, in the sacraments of the church and the life of sanctification, it is the Spirit who joins us to the Son and only God can join us to God, then the Spirit, too, must be God in this wholly consubstantial sense. In Christ, they believed, God in his fullness really has come to dwell in our midst; and in the Holy Spirit, God in his fullness has really brought us to dwell in Christ. Thus, when we turn to the great exponents of Nicene theology in the fourth century, what we find in their texts is not merely a catechetical recitation of received wisdom but also a patient practice of critical anamnesis, a discipline of recollection that is also a synthesis of the full testimony of the past. Perhaps the most perfect example of this is Basil of Caesarea's *On the Holy Spirit*, which argued as forcibly as possible—without overstepping the language of Scripture or the Nicene creed—for the full divinity of the Holy Spirit, against all doubters. Of course, the Spirit is nowhere clearly called either *ho theos* or *theos* in the New Testament; and Basil's treatise nowhere violates this rule of reticence (if that is what it is). It was left up to Gregory of Nazianzus, in his *Five Theological Orations*, to extend the boundaries of the received vocabulary and boldly to proclaim the full divinity of the Spirit. But Basil's text is fascinating for its sheer systematic comprehensiveness. It lays out a survey of the whole of Scripture as well as the most venerable liturgical usages of the church, and it constructs a marvelously, even seemingly overwhelming case for the Godhead of the Spirit. And every step is governed by a single compelling question: What do Christians mean when they say that they have been saved in and by Christ by the power of the Holy Spirit? By the end, Basil's case—and there simply is no more systematic treatment of the issue in patristic literature—powerfully suggests that only the full "homo-ousian" Trinitarian position makes it possible to view Christian belief as a coherent vision of God's action in Christ. And indeed, by comparison to Basil's exposition of the faith, the Arian and Eunomian positions do seem to dissolve into fragmentary and contradictory mythologies. That may be only an appearance, admittedly—we know of the anti-Nicene party only through the reports of their adversaries—but Basil's accomplishment was an astonishing one in any event. On the one hand, his argument was in no sense procrustean or artificial—he truly drew on the language and beliefs and inherent logic of the Christian past—but, on the other, it was the result of a boldly creative interpretive labor. The tradition he described was arguably really already there in some sense, if one could piece it together in just the right way; but it required that piecing together as well as a considerable degree of filtering out useless pieces, and when the picture was complete, it still constituted something startling and new, something that made the familiar strange. This same question of salvation, moreover, drove the christological disputes of the following centuries and prompted the same kind of inspired syntheses. It could not have been otherwise.

What does all of this have to do with tradition as such, however? Simply enough, any true and living tradition must be at once both the subject and the object of a constant and pious hermeneutical retrieval that, guided by an awareness of the history and logic of what has gone before, seeks to discover the tradition's dialectical unity and rationality ever anew. And thus openness to an unanticipated future is no less necessary than fidelity to the past. The Arians and Eunomians and their religious kith were, when all was said and done, the theological conservatives of their time and place; the members of the Nicene party were the daring innovators, willing to break with the past in order to preserve its spiritual force. The former were traditionalists, and for that reason their language ultimately proved sterile; the latter were theological and metaphysical radicals, and as a consequence their language gave the tradition new and enduring life.

TRADITION'S SECRETS

It is only *by way of tradition*—as a passage through time, that is, as a transmission, as the impartation of a gift that remains sealed, as a giving always deferred toward a future not yet known—that the secret inner presence *in tradition* can be made manifest at all. Only in the ceaseless flow of its intertwining variations can the theme subtending the whole music be heard. And in part this is because whatever is imparted must be received in the mode of the recipient, with all his or her limitations and possibilities. In the end, after all, the historical and cultural contingencies of a tradition also constitute the vehicle of its passage through the ages. They are its flesh and blood in any given epoch, its necessary embodiment within the intelligible structures of concrete existence. Without those contingencies, the animating impulse of the tradition would be something less than a ghost. But by the same token, once that vital force has moved on to assume new living configurations, the unnatural attempt to preserve the earlier forms can produce nothing but a painted cadaver. Hence, true fidelity to whatever is most original and most final in a tradition requires a positive desire for moments of dissolution just as much as for passages of recapitulation and refrain. And the hermeneutical labor needed to understand any tradition requires disruption no less than stability, "progressive" ambition no less than "conservative" prudence, because it is only through the play of tension and resolution, of stability and disintegration, that that which is most imperishable in a tradition can be fitfully perceived—or at least sensed. But alas, there is no single formula for doing this well or any simple method for avoiding misunderstanding. Such rules of interpretation as there are can never be more than general and rather fluid guidelines. They cannot even provide us, when we consult the witness of history, with a dependable scale of proportionality. It is quite possible (and on occasion it has happened) that even the most devout interpreter or community of interpreters, in looking back to the initial moments of the tradition and their immediate sequels and consequences, might reasonably conclude that the overwhelming preponderance of Christian history—its practices, presuppositions, civic orders, governing values, reigning pieties—have amounted to little more than a sustained apostasy from the apostolic exemplars of the church. That hidden source of the tradition's life remains a real and unyielding standard, not a majority consensus, and before its judgment, even the most venerable of institutional inheritances may have to fall away. And yet, by the very same token, it remains hidden in the very act of judgment, and thus can be the exclusive property of no individual or age. Anyone who arrogates to himself the power to say with absolute finality what the *one true* tradition is will invariably prove something of a fool and usually something of a thug. We see this today, for instance, among the fiercest of Pope Francis's traditionalist detractors: in how absurdly their hostility exceeds any provocation he has given them, in how eagerly and opportunistically they pounce upon any chance misunderstanding, rumor, or vicious distortion that serves their polemical purposes, and in how staggeringly ignorant they are of the larger Catholic tradition they imagine they are defending. It is all too obvious that what they find most insufferable about him is his commitment to understanding the demands of the gospel rather than to shoring up the ramparts of the early modern institutions of the Roman communion;

what offends them is his Christianity. (This is hardly surprising, I suppose; it seems altogether probable that these same religious traditionalists, were Jesus to appear in their midst, would want to see him crucified for the sake of the faith.) But again, to find the safe middle passage between the Scylla and Charybdis of a destructively pure originalism and a degenerate traditionalism, one must rely not on any particular method; one must instead simply attempt to practice a certain kind of hermeneutical piety. Tacit knowledge, faithful practice, humility before the testimony of the generations, prayerfulness, and any number of moral and intellectual virtues are required; but these can be cultivated only in being put into practice. In a very real sense, in fact, this is what "tradition" is when considered as a hermeneutical practice: an attitude of trusting skepticism, hesitant impetuosity; a certain critical hygiene of prudent reluctance, a certain devotion to the limitless fecundity of the tradition's initiating moment or original principle, a certain trusting surrender to a future that cannot alter what has been but that might nevertheless alter one's understanding of the past both radically and irrevocably. It is the conviction that one has truly heard a call from the realm of the transcendent, but a call that must be heard again before its meaning can be grasped or its summons obeyed; and the labor of interpretation is the diligent practice of waiting attentively in the interval, for fear otherwise of forgetting the tone and content of that first vocation.

In a sense, a tradition reveals its secrets only through moments of disruption precisely because it is itself, in its very essence, a disruption: it begins entirely as a *novum*, an unanticipated awakening to something hitherto unknown, and one that requires the entirety of history then to interpret. The wise believer cultivates hermeneutical patience before disruptions of practice or confession or self-understanding, not merely as a matter of tolerance or indulgence but in order to be capable of a genuine attempt to recapture in the present something of the force of that initial displacement of normal expectations from which his or her tradition arose—that first event that set loose the "line of flight" to which the believer belongs. This is the only true faithfulness to the memory of an absolute beginning, without precedent: an empty tomb, say, or the voice of God heard in rolling thunder or inscribed on the wind in letters of fire. One might even say that a tradition exists only as a sustained apocalypse, a moment of pure awakening preserved as at once an ever dissolving recollection and an ever renewed surprise. And so any truly faithful hermeneutical return to the origin of a tradition is the renewal of a moment of revolution, and the very act of return is itself a kind of revolutionary venture that, ever and again, is willing to break with the conventional forms of the fleeting present in order to serve that deeper truth. What makes a tradition live is that holy thing within that can be neither seen nor touched, which dwells within a sanctuary into which the faithful cannot peer but demands their service nevertheless. To return to the source is to approach the veil of the Holy of Holies, to draw near once again to the presence upon the other side, even sometimes to enter in—though then only to find that the presence remains invisible or hidden in a blaze of glory or an impenetrable cloud.

In this way, tradition sets us free. In a sense, every living tradition constitutes a sovereign apocalyptic exception to the reign of pure history or (better) bare history: history, that is, understood as a chronicle of sheer consecutive causality, interminable eventuality as such, without term or final cause or import; the history whose only measure and meaning is death. History thus conceived, thus denuded of all the trappings of great epic or drama or dialectical process, without a secret to be disclosed or a rationale to be comprehended or a consummation to be awaited, is the ultimate prison of the rational spirit. And so—just as the reiterations and returns of ritual and liturgy displace the empty flow of time with a closed circle of "completed" time, timeless time, the living eternity of joyous repetition—so also living traditions gather up the moments for us altogether differently, rise above the ceaseless empty flow of bare history, shape all things toward a final truth, and thus displace the rule of bare history with the adventure of a coherent journey through the ages, from a remote beginning to a remote end. Tradition is in a sense the diachronic complement of ritual's periodic synchrony; it is history as always inflected by a force from outside time's continuum: history moving forward but with each of its moments bearing an oblique stress that pulls it toward something not confined to time. It is for this reason that no living tradition can be properly understood merely as a precious inheritance to be protected and curated. Even the act of reverently looking back through the past to a tradition's origin is also an act of critique, a judgment on the past that need not be a kind one, as well as an implicit act of submission to a future verdict that might be equally unkind with regard to the present, and even to a final verdict in whose light all the forms a tradition encompasses can be understood as at best provisional intimations of something ineffable and inconceivable. A tradition's life is this irrepressible apocalyptic ferment within, beckoning us simultaneously back to an immemorial past and forward to an unimaginable future. The proper moral and spiritual attitude to a tradition's formal expressions, then, is not a simple clinging to what has been received but also a relinquishing—even, at times, of things that had once seemed most precious: *Gelassenheit,* to use Meister Eckhart's language, release. Only thus can one receive tradition as a liberating counter-history, as the apocalyptic exception to bare history that promises us a higher truth than death: by remembering a first interruption, awaiting a last interruption, and attempting to sustain the theme uniting them in the interval. Only thus can one find the meaninglessness of bare history converted into a completed tale of vocation and judgment, of a call heard from far away that nevertheless summons one to a promised homeland. Perhaps, of course, the entire tale is an illusion at the end of the day, a fable we have told ourselves to carry us through the dark places of this world. Conversely, though, perhaps tradition comes to us instead as an entirely gracious invasion of history, shattering the walls of our prison: a gift awakening us (if we will listen) to the knowledge that the *kenoma* of bare history is not our true home, and that our true story comes from—and must finally be told—elsewhere.

4

Disruptions and Connections

Rediscovering and Remaking the Muslim Tradition in Late Modernity

Ebrahim Moosa
University of Notre Dame

PRACTITIONERS AND STUDENTS OF religion recognize that contemporary religious practices and beliefs were once part of a different world. But the past and the present always have a complex relationship with one another. This is what makes the study of tradition and its transmission interesting. Aspects of a tradition might be continuous with the past, discontinuous with it, or part of a complex set of overlapping cosmologies representing both past and present. Tradition, furthermore, is always shaped by particular economic and political milieus with their own arts, literatures, histories, liturgies, and moral practices—all of which are tied to a particular conception of being-in-the-world. With the devout of other traditions, Muslims usually have commitments to long-observed practices and outlooks, even if they might struggle with some aspects of their tradition. Some might silently wonder if some of these practices still apply today and whether or not selected ones are mutable. Others are inclined to accept dutifully what has been handed down, while still others might vocally challenge past practices and advocate reforms.

Thinking about tradition can raise difficult questions. If tradition is mutable, then what are the limits of alteration and remaking it? If it is unchangeable, then why and how does one engage with it when it appears anachronistic? These are age-old questions, but periodically, they come to us in new forms.

In the cultural climate of late modernity, such questions have become acute for Muslims. Forces of globalization, which have spread Western intellectual and religious currents of thought to the Islamic world, have often led to intense discussions among Muslims about the state, future, and present-day applicability of their traditions. Internecine divisions have arisen among Muslims, pitting adherents of different sub-traditions against one another. Perhaps the most transformative encounter leading to our current moment took place when multiple Muslim societies came under the political control and intellectual sway of modern European colonial powers in the eighteenth and nineteenth centuries.

This essay explores aspects of this encounter, especially its intellectual implications for contemporary Muslim thought and practice. But first, we will consider the meaning of tradition more probingly, drawing from past commentary and reckoning with three contemporary thinkers: Aziz al-Azmeh and Fahmī Jad'ān (whom I engage constructively) and the late Saba Mahmood (whom I criticize). Toward the end of the chapter, we will turn to the thought of Ibn Khaldūn (1332–1406), a particularly valuable conversation partner, I shall contend, for Muslims today who desire to think incisively and imaginatively about the question of tradition. Along the way, I think one will observe how debates over tradition among Muslims today resemble disputes that have taken place within Judaism and Christianity in the recent past.

TRADITION: TAKING A CLOSER LOOK

Tradition is an abstract concept in Arabic-Islamic thought and it is often deployed in confusing ways. Its meanings range from the "past" in general, to "religious doctrines," to "Islam in its totality." Many people speak freely about "traditional perspectives." These perspectives bring with them value judgments and they generate particular social and political practices and commitments; sometimes they might even "devalue" the past or create a "rupture" with it, albeit in the name of tradition. Further, tradition might stand more prosaically for customary institutions, actions, ideas, and written and oral texts from the past, which are accepted as normative for a given community.[1]

Particular words matter and they can be difficult to translate. In debates concerning tradition in an Arabic/Muslim context, one sometimes encounters "legacy" (turāth), "canonical tradition in law or normativity" (madhhab), or "that which is 'given' or provided in a path" (shar' or shar'īyāt), among other vocabularies. Their use and the context in which they are used can spark debates about the meaning of traditions.[2]

In recent decades, discussions among Muslims about tradition have often found food for thought in the Western academy. Particular noteworthy are the reflections on tradition offered by the philosopher Alasdair MacIntyre. His ideas, in turn, have shaped conversations among social scientists and anthropologists, notably Talal Asad, who study Muslim societies "on the ground" and not just Muslims' learned traditions. Such anthropological and sociological studies have invigorated debates about tradition in interesting ways.[3]

To reflect on tradition more intently, let's turn briefly to the extraordinary medieval figure, Abū Ḥāmid al-Ghazālī (d. 1111). In a memorable passage, he reminds us about two sources of learning and thinking that are indispensable to each other: reason or intellect ('aql) and that which is learned through auditory means, literally "heard" (sam'), or what is sometimes called the transmitted tradition. "The intellect," he writes, "cannot dispense with instruction transmitted by hearing nor can instruction transmitted by hearing dispense with the intellect."[4] Transmission by hearing and audition has a simple formulation in Arabic—the word samā'—but it contains an entire universe of meaning. Ideas, teachings, habits, practices were transmitted intergenerationally for centuries by means of the spoken and heard word, in short reenacting what is heard, observed, and

1. I want to thank Thomas Albert Howard for his careful edits and suggestions in this chapter. I thank Mahmoud Youness for the research support provided for this chapter.
   For a brief overview of "tradition" in recent Islam, see Graham, "Traditionalism in Islam."

2. See Kendall and Khan, Reclaiming Islamic Tradition. For an excellent and close study of how scholars engage tradition see Haj, Reconfiguring Islamic Tradition; Jad'ān, Naẓarīyat al-turāth wa-dirāsāt 'Arabīya wa-Islāmīya ukhra.

3. See, for example, Asad, "Thinking about Tradition."

4. Al-Ghazālī, Iḥyā' 'ulūm al-dīn, 3:17; Kitāb sharḥ 'ajā'ib al-qalb, 48.

understood. That hearing component, the ear, then often functions as a synecdoche for what is called tradition in Islam. In one constellation of words—listening and recitation—an entire civilization of hearing and performance is portrayed. One outcome is the role of orality in Arabicate cultures, namely, the need for "direct control of learning by the agencies and institutions of learning" and to prevent "the unmediated access to sources."[5] Only centuries later, with the advent of written culture, was the oral tradition transformed into one of notation and documentation. But even then, "hearing" had an abidingly important place in Muslim tradition: the written word did not displace but rather even sought to simulate older oral practices in a new medium.

Another category embedded in the learned traditions of Islam is the idea of a lived community practice, known as the *sunna*. Containing both good and bad elements, this in fact preceded Islam.[6] With the advent of Islam, this lived practice gradually became consecrated as the exemplary practice of the Prophet Muhammad and often turned out to be an important source of Islamic teaching. Yet the concept of tradition continued to grow in Muslim history as other forms of passing down critical learning and practices were cultivated over time.[7] Multiple specialized fields developed—law, theology, literature, and history, among others. These shaped and added variety to the tradition. In many respects, tradition became synonymous with so-called "reports" from these fields. The authenticity of reports, secured through a chain of narrators (*isnād*, pl. *asānīd*), became at once theaters for the transmission of tradition and the tradition itself.

The Syrian-born scholar Aziz al-Azmeh, perhaps more than anyone, has raised critical questions about understandings of tradition in Arab-Islamic societies, which owes their origins to the seventh century and to later developments in Arabicate and Persianate cultures.[8] Tradition is regularly secured through pedagogic techniques, which hallow the origins of the tradition as incontrovertible—what Azmeh calls "apodictic."[9] Based on hierarchy, companionship, and apprenticeship, these apodictic techniques lead to a partial mystification of pedagogic authority and a veneration of the learned fields and disciplines of the tradition. Teachers and authors

5. Al-Azmeh, *Arabic Thought and Islamic Societies*, 234.

6. Juynboll and Brown, "Sunna."

7. Valliere, "Tradition."

8. Al-Azmeh, *Arabic Thought and Islamic Societies*, 228–38.

9. Al-Azmeh, *Arabic Thought and Islamic Societies*, 229.

themselves are not the sources of authority, but over time, they come to serve as the revered mouthpieces of a complex "epistemic and legislative oracle," as Azmeh puts it.[10] Although the origins of disciplines are taken to be beyond doubt, anchored in a mythical *Urtext*, Azmeh nonetheless raises sharp questions—questions often occluded by the cumulative weight of the tradition. After problematizing the sources of tradition, Azmeh acknowledges that traditions of learning are nonetheless effectively transmitted due to the aforementioned techniques of pedagogy, which induce in the student a skill-creating process of training (*habitus/malaka*).[11] But even if these methods are effective, Azmeh worries that they often bring about the "closure" of each discipline and science; students only hallow them and they are not taught how to creatively engage with them. "Closure of sciences," writes Azmeh, "is realized . . . by its faithful transmission . . . with the affirmation of a tradition by means of its constant redaction and as present in the institution through which learning is borne."[12] Put differently, the authority of tradition is not *historically preserved* but rather *ritually preserved* through processes of education and initiation. In order to allow for historical transmission, Azmeh believes that one must recognize that "it is always the present which constitutes the past after its own image" or that the past is best and most faithfully preserved in terms of the requirements and imperatives of the present. Absent such a recognition, Azmeh feels that the past will only be beheld and not employed, thus turning the present into the passive recipient of the past, not a dynamic participant in the making of tradition. Commenting more generally on the Islamic past as tradition, Azmeh writes: "It is not the past, 'tradition,' that lives in the present, but it is rather the present which reclaims that past, and this has never been done except very selectively, ever renewing it, but always attributing this reclamation and renewal to the past itself, and undertaking it in the name of the past. . . . The integrity of tradition is a myth of origin articulated in many forms, as logical or exemplary apodicticity, as positive origins; it is a myth which unifies a culture by provision of a uniform sphere of reference in terms of which, by means of education, paradigms are differentiated."[13]

These are of course complex matters, and Azmeh's prose is sometimes more suggestive than precise. Whatever the case, the idea of tradition has

10. Al-Azmeh, *Arabic Thought and Islamic Societies*, 229.

11. Al-Azmeh, *Arabic Thought and Islamic Societies*, 233.

12. Al-Azmeh, *Arabic Thought and Islamic Societies*, 237.

13. Al-Azmeh, *Arabic Thought and Islamic Societies*, 237.

been widely debated in modern times as Muslim communities have sought to carve out identities and futures for themselves in a post-colonial world greatly influenced by the West. In this regard, we will turn to another contemporary scholar, Fahmī Jad'ān, a Jordan-based Palestinian historian of Islamic philosophy, who sees tradition as essentially constituted by "human accomplishments"; it is the product of human endeavor and creativity.[14] In making this claim, Jad'ān makes a distinction between theology and metaphysics on the one hand and the human understanding and approximation of them on the other. Yes, knowledge of the Qur'ān as Scripture and knowledge about the teachings of the prophet Muḥammad are the bedrock of much Muslim thought and practice. But the actual teachings of the sacred are not in themselves identical with tradition. The sacred is always filtered through human approximation and the creation and development of a variety of discursive practices. Jad'ān is among the few scholars who, along with Azmeh, makes such a clear distinction between the two. But in doing so, he has helped distinguish between the sacred itself and the many-faceted, human-created discursive traditions that have sought to interpret it and realize it over time.

Jad'ān emphasizes that tradition understood as heritage, turāth, is a double-edged sword. Together with the many positive aspects of tradition also come the problematic aspects: "authority, monarchy, and sacrality," i.e., the coercive dimensions of tradition.[15] Arab-Islamic tradition, in Jad'ān's view, is tethered to three crucial relationships: a relationship with religion, with Arabness or Arab nationalism, and with humanism.[16] We might also think of these as different pillars or strands. The role of Islam as a religio-civilizational force is undeniable, but debates continually arise between those who give Islam and its accomplishments a significant but limited role in the formation of the Arab-Islamic tradition and those who see Islam as virtually tantamount to the tradition itself. The latter camp over-sacralizes the tradition, and this enchantment or "sacrality" (qadāsa), argues Jad'ān, has at times haunted the Islamic tradition. Arab nationalism, too, has a stake in the Islamic heritage, since the Arabs, beginning in the seventh century and in locations of present-day Saudi Arabia, played such a crucial role in shaping the consciousness of the people who identified with Islam. But neither religious commitment nor national/ethnic identity exhaust the

14. Jad'ān, Naẓarīyat al-turāth.
15. Jad'ān, Naẓarīyat al-turāth, 13 ("al-sulṭa, al-qasr, al-qadāsa").
16. Jad'ān, Naẓarīyat al-turāth, 14.

Arab-Islamic tradition. Arabic people and their faith have contributed to the broader story of humanity. Put differently, the Arabic heritage is not for Arabs alone but a tradition for all of humanity to learn from, to grapple with. This is what Jadʿān means by humanism, and along with faith and ethnicity, it is a third "relation" or pillar of Islamic civilization in his interpretation.[17]

Tradition is not something abstract for Jadʿān. It is always dynamic in its "embodied this-ness"; that is, it has "political" significance, and as a consequence, it is "social" and can be "ideological."[18] Jadʿān points out that when tradition comes under the purview of ideology, it usually takes one of three forms: people either become (1) hidebound literalists (*salafiyūn taqlīdiyūn*), attempting to realize the sacred apart and separate from discursive reasoning and reflection; they become (2) revolutionaries without a sense of the absolute that can relativize and constrain their own endeavors; or they become (3) selective and eclectic constructivists, accepting this and rejecting that aspect of a tradition in the absence of clear epistemological agreement among all parties to a tradition. Each one of these positions reflect the exigencies and configurations of power arrangements in a given society, according to Jadʿān.

Additionally, one of two approaches in conversations about tradition are available to us, argues Jadʿān. One is to accept tradition as having a "natural place," passively embracing and trying to understand it in its three relations: religion, Arabness, and humanism. The second approach commits one to what he calls "realist pragmatism."[19] Such pragmatism, which entails discrimination, helps one decide which elements of these relations ought to be retained in order to constitute a flourishing and functioning tradition. Often those elements that have withstood the test of time will define the final meaning of tradition.[20] Jadʿān is wary of idealized conceptions of "reviving" or "drawing inspiration" from tradition. In his interpretation, these moves can easily become anachronistic and mechanistic—if not downright flawed and fruitless—modes of engagement with tradition. What is more, they can prevent one from constructively engaging with new cultural and civilizational developments in the present. They often sacrifice nuance for artificial certainty. Nonetheless, tradition should also not be defined by grabbing whatever pleases us from the past and dressing it

17. Jadʿān, *Naẓariyat al-turāth*, 14.
18. Jadʿān, *Naẓariyat al-turāth*, 14 ("al-annī al-mushakhkhaṣ").
19. "wāqiʿīya ʿamalīya."
20. Jadʿān, *Naẓariyat al-turāth*, 15.

up to suit what fits well with our contemporary sentiments. In contrast to idealizing the past and over-accommodation to the present, Jad'ān believes that one should first pause and observe how a tradition has been lived out and is being lived out. Such an "experiential" approach to tradition works against investing it with fanciful, erroneous conceptions, even if it also has the potential to demystify the assumed "sacrality" attached to tradition. Experiential familiarity with a tradition, in other words, helps "ground" it in actuality and staves off overly sentimental or romanticized understandings of it.

Further, Jad'ān favors a creative engagement with tradition and, invoking a metaphor from biological chemistry, he proposes viewing tradition as an "organic or living compound," one that grows and develops over time, that even "metabolizes."[21] Such a biological paradigm finds sustenance from three sources: firstly, actual involvement in a lived tradition (as mentioned); secondly, a discriminating discursive mindset to reflect on the given realities surrounding the Muslim community; and thirdly, sacred sources or revelation. Of these three sources perhaps one and three come most naturally: drawing from revelation and involvement in an actual community of practitioners. But two is equally important. One must have the discursive ability, the perspicacity, to reflect on and evaluate what one is doing. This reflective or "psychological" aspect is critical because it gives the practitioner discerning acumen and a sensibility of past achievement, thus helping him or her deal with challenges, defeats, and setbacks.[22] Additionally, beauty is required, for without aesthetics—literature, art, architecture, music, and the fine arts—tradition is impoverished. Beauty elevates us from isolation and small-mindedness, replenishing the spiritual resources of a person, community, and a people.[23] All literary and aesthetic elements must undergo a "figurative metabolism" just as all disciplines of knowledge are part of this metabolizing process as well.[24] Taken together, these aspects of a tradition contain both practical and contemplative resources, which have historically sustained communities.

A living tradition, Jad'ān emphasizes, is not static: some aspects continue over time and are incorporated into the ongoing present while others wither away and drop out. For this reason, one must always exercise

21. Jad'ān, Naẓariyat al-turāth, 31 ("al-murakkab al-ḥayy").

22. Jad'ān, Naẓariyat al-turāth, 30.

23. Jad'ān, Naẓariyat al-turāth, 30.

24. Jad'ān, Naẓariyat al-turāth, 34–36 ("istiqlāb ma'nawī").

discretion, avoiding elements of a tradition that violate human dignity or detract from human flourishing. In making his proposals, Jad'ān is fully aware of the unequal and disproportionate power of the West in shaping knowledge about and reflection on tradition. And he concedes that some Muslims might dissent from his views. But the challenge to participate in the formation of an innovative and vital Muslim tradition remains as inviting as it is difficult, and one should neither walk away from the opportunity nor seek succor in too-simplistic solutions.

***

Modern Islam encounters the inherited or transmitted tradition in at least two discursive contexts. To politically secular and nationalist advocates among Muslim and Christian segments of Arabic-speaking societies, tradition presents itself as part of a sequence of renewals (*tajdīd*) of tradition (*turāth*).[25] Jad'ān aligns with this camp, but not if the idea of renewal is a surreptitious way of importing atavistic and regressive ideas as a stand-in for tradition. Others employ "renewal" in a more emphatically religious way. Given the semantic breadth behind "renewal," the term has taken on a larger meaning over time, that of a civilizational renewal.[26] But it also bears a more secular connotation in the modern period as indigenous cultural renewal against the foreign hegemony of Western powers. Renewal draws its strength from the religious vocabulary of Islam, particularly in regard to the prophecy of Muhammad that God would send a person every hundred years to renew *dīn*, too often translated uncritically as "religion" in modern times, but in fact meaning the idea of the good, the truly normative, the salvific order for society.

Politically secular Muslims have latched on to the idea of renewal as being synonymous with the revitalization of culture and sometimes they intend by renewal the "enlightenment" of Arab-Islamic civilization.[27] Secular voices employ *turāth*, literally meaning that which "remained,"[28] but when they do so they use it to signify the attainment of a cosmopolitan civilizational advancement. Such usage of the term might not be hostile to

25. See Ḥanafī, *Al-Turāth wa-al-tajdīd*.

26. Moosa and Tareen, "Revival and Reform."

27. Al-Jābirī and Dowell, *Arab-Islamic Philosophy*.

28. Al-Khalīl ibn Aḥmad al-Farāhīdī, *Kitāb al-'Ayn*, 4:362.

religion, but it does not give religion an exclusive or decisive role in determining normative judgments and/or cultural values and sensibilities.

By contrast, in the religious circles of Arabic-speaking societies as well as in different parts of the non-Arabic speaking world where Muslim-majority societies and minority communities prevail, a different set of vocabularies and valences are deployed to grapple with quandaries posed by tradition and its renewal. In these circles, debates are usually most intense concerning what counts as Muslim ethics or what might be categorized as "Islamic law." Debates over tradition usually pit those who permit human authority *ab initio* to initiate an interpretive framework (*ijtihād*) in order to discover norms for juridical and moral scholarship against those who oppose such efforts and who call for religiously-inspired normative scholarship to strictly adhere to the unmolested authority (*taqlīd*) of tradition. Polarized positions in this matter—especially in Sunnī circles, but to a lesser extent in Shīʿa quarters—have often resulted in mutual antagonism and stalemate. Some conciliation has been arrived at once the assumptions and goals of various positions have been sufficiently examined. But many modernizing voices continue to regard *taqlīd*, which they see as an appeal to authority without soliciting proof in support of their arguments, as the permanent adversary of their bid to perform *ijtihad*. Thus, one often encounters a relentless and unhelpful polarization, pitting *taqlīd* against *ijtihad*, without any compromise or forward movement.

Yet a third trend is found in the literary realm of Arabic letters, both in the premodern and modern eras. A particularly relevant figure is the contemporary Syrian poet and literary critic Ali Ahmad Saʿīd (b. 1930), better known by his pen name Adūnīs or Adonis. In his four-volume work *The Permanent and the Changeable*, he lays the blames for the lack of innovation and creativity in Arabic letters squarely on the notion of formality and hidebound conformity (*taqlīd*).[29] One of the more exciting developments spurred by Adonis and others is a return to the idea of *adab* (plural, *ādāb*) as a "field of production" to invoke a formula associated with the French critic Pierre Bourdieu.[30] *Adab* is the term for literature but the same term can be used for ethics. Historically viewed, *adab* suggests a field of normativity not strictly beholden to religiously-inspired normativity, found more in the realms of culture, civilization, and experience. This field was never understood to stand apart from religious influence—and a major figure such as

29. Adūnīs, *al-Thābit wa-al-mutaḥawwil*.
30. Bourdieu, *Field of Cultural Production*, 9.

al-Ghazālī employs it in a religious sense—but it did alternate between a certain autonomy from the religious field and at times even a dialectical relationship with this field. To rejuvenate the conversation about tradition in Islam today and search for premodern models, the notion of *adab* is and will continue to be a vital resource provided the historical present is viewed as an active dimension in the making of tradition. Debates on the meaning, purpose, and relevance of tradition are ongoing. They produce both exciting and at times soul-searing predicaments for communities and individuals; they have resulted in both tragic elements of loss and creative moments of gain.

TRADITION AND THE (LATE) MODERN PREDICAMENT

In contemporary Muslim discourse, the debate about tradition, to my mind, has received insufficient historical and theoretical scrutiny since passions and politics often preclude coherent conversation and considered judgment. For instance, in some Western scholarly circles, the Muslim engagement with Aristotelian thought is seen, and welcomed, as a novelty. Yet in Islamic history, Aristotle and Aristotelianism, as well as Platonism, were long considered fixtures in philosophy, theology, law, and literature. Even so, perhaps the return to Aristotle, especially after Alasdair MacIntyre's strong appeal to this figure, is, for some, an appropriate response to modernity, since his thought offers a capacious space for inquiry and reflection relevant to multiple communities of discourse. But in my judgement, this remains insufficient. Recall the dilemma Jadʿān points us to concerning the hegemony of Western liberalism and the challenges that this poses for the production of a creative and imaginative Muslim engagement with tradition in the present. Questions of power and competing ideologies around the world complicate Muslims' efforts to engage tradition creatively and produces a climate best characteized by the Greek notion of agonism—perpetual struggle.

To illustrate what I mean, let's focus on the anthropologist Saba Mahmood, who made significant contributions on gender, religion, and secularity before her untimely death in 2018. In an important essay, she offers an acute analysis of the foolhardy efforts of the US government and US-based think tanks to propose reforms for Islam.[31] But her essay quickly

31. Mahmood, "Secularism, Hermeneutics, and Empire."

loses all nuance when she appears to suggest that there is collusion between US policy aims and what she deems as "liberal" currents of thought in the Muslim world. She argues that post-9/11 US policy toward the Islamic world is coterminous with the fruit of decades of work by leading secular and left-leaning literary scholars and philosophers of Islamic thought; she even names Naṣr Ḥāmid Abū Zayd (d. 2010) and Ḥasan Ḥanafī from Egypt and the reformist intellectual Abdul Karim Soroush from Iran as unwitting collaborators with US policy. Bear in mind that these intellectuals sought to further the modern Arab renaissance (*nahḍa*) in the case of the two Egyptians or to voice dissent with post-revolutionary Iran in the case of Soroush. Mahmood astonishingly attempts to show that these intellectuals and their followers were wittingly or unwittingly bedfellows of a nefarious US agenda to manufacture and export liberal Islam to the world. She made this claim despite the fact that all three scholars were critical of US policies before and after 9/11 and hardly self-identified as liberal!

Mahmood fails to show common threads between these Muslim intellectuals and the US government and other US actors (especially the secularism-touting and security-oriented Rand Corporation), yet she reaches the questionable conclusion that the two sides in fact share common political ends, namely, to remake Islam in the image of Western liberalism and secularism. Even worse, she seemed to suggest that reformers must also carry the burden of US imperial designs. As she put it, the "US strategists have struck a common chord with self-identified liberal Muslim reformers who have been trying to refashion Islam along the lines of the Protestant Reformation."[32] No names of well-known figures with whom the US government have struck "a common chord" are mentioned in her essay, but these two Egyptians and Iranian are named and implicated in an apparent collusion.

What Mahmood omits saying is that the intellectual efforts, especially of Ḥanafī and Abū Zayd, began decades ago in left-inspired readings of traditional literary, philosophical, and theological resources. But for Mahmood, what counted was that after the 9/11 attacks, attempts were made to "reform Islam" by the US government and its allies. Her strategy was to rename critical Muslim intellectuals as "liberal" without any validation. By suggesting guilt by association, an entire archive of scholarship unrelated to these political designs now suddenly becomes tainted by being seen as in service to the American project. "The convergence," she writes, "of US

---

32. Mahmood, "Secularism, Hermeneutics, and Empire," 329.

imperial interests and the secular liberal Muslim agenda needs to be understood, therefore, not simply as a fortuitous coming together of political objectives and an indigenous social formation, but . . . from the standpoint of normative secularity and the kind of religious subjectivity it endorses."[33] Again, Mahmood omits to tell her readers that varieties of liberal Islam have at least a century-old pedigree in the Muslim world, long pre-dating recent US foreign policy interests. One wonders how far back Mahmood would have pushed her argument and whom she would implicate in the roster of prosecutable actors for being part of this "convergence" of US "imperial interests" and a "secular liberal Muslim agenda."[34]

She accuses Soroush for saying that revelation is "silent." Yet she shows no awareness that Soroush was merely channeling ʿAlī b. Abū Ṭālib, the first leader after the Prophet Muḥammad, an imām, in terms of Shīʿa theological claims and the fourth Sunni caliph. ʿAlī is reported to have rebuked persons who used unfiltered Qurʾānic passages as political slogans. The Qurʾān, ʿAlī remarkably said, was between two covers, and it is men who interpret it. Would Mahmood's "convergence" of ideas also implicate the eleventh-century al-Ghazālī? The latter built on the readings of his teacher and formulated a utilitarian theory of the purposes of the Sharīʿa, the normative rules of Islam. In doing so, Ghazālī initiated an entirely new outcome-based reading of Sharīʿa that has gained great traction in modern times. In other words, to use one of Mahmood's keywords, Ghazali "resituated" enormous tracts of scholarship in formulating his argument and hermeneutic. The ill-advised nature of Mahmood's prosecution is patent and cannot survive close scrutiny. But perhaps even more astonishing is that her harsh judgment on these scholars went largely unchallenged. To be fair, her essay contains a salutary critique of US-based agencies and of Western secularism, which often functions as *ersatz*-religion in her view. Yet these positive elements do not detract from the disservice that she does to critical Muslim thought by conflating it with US foreign policy and liberalism.

I particularly disagree with Mahmood for wading into hermeneutical complexities of the historical tradition of Islamic thought and for allowing over-confidence in her political convictions to run roughshod over circumspection. In doing so, she exploited a sensitive and contentious zone of intra-Muslim debate on questions of interpretation, authority, and the meaning of a religious tradition in modernity, in order to serve her political

33. Mahmood, "Secularism, Hermeneutics, and Empire," 329.
34. Mahmood, "Secularism, Hermeneutics, and Empire," 329.

ends, filled, as they are, with presentism and as an indulgence toward questionable ultra-orthodox Muslim practices that she condoned in a previous book, *Politics of Piety*, as almost the totality of authentic Islam.[35]

Muslim orthodoxy of different stripes zealously guards and polices the boundaries of allowable interpretation. Its ammunition includes proclamations of heresy and excommunication; these are not simple admonitions but rather are meant to target and discredit thinkers such as Abū Zayd or Soroush. If Muslim orthodoxy's criticism stopped at the mere denouncement of rivals' views, that would be a mercy. But these denunciations are often accompanied by edict-like fatwas that encourage violence against those labeled reformers, critics, or freethinkers. Mahmood's unjustified association of critical Muslim thinkers with American imperialism only plays to the choir of these unsavory aspects of Muslim orthodoxy and its violent allies in various geographical theaters.

Mahmood's intervention distorts an accurate view of Islamic reform; where it required nuance, she offers a blanket attempt to discredit efforts at rethinking Muslim religious thought and tradition. In her view, reformers were attempting to "resituate" religious texts.[36] And this amounted to an attempt to frame Islam within a despised modality of modern liberalism or, worse, within a hermeneutics of American empire; whether her targets intended to have a dalliance with American power was irrelevant.[37] In her own words:

> What is notable here is that these liberal reformers do not abandon the religious text but resituate it. The question is, once metaphysical intention is separated from the text, how is this text to be read and what would its significance be for the secularized believer? The liberal reformers are resolute in their answer, as is the Rand Corporation report: the Quran should be read as a system of signs and symbols, whose meaning is to be deciphered in a manner not dissimilar to how we read literature or poetry—its meaning open to infinite play but also to historical determination. The notion of the transcendent, no longer locatable within the religious text, finds a place in the ineffable and privatized world of individual readers who turn not to traditional authority but to their own cultured sensibilities to experience the true meaning of the word.[38]

35. Mahmood, *Politics of Piety*.
36. Mahmood, "Secularism, Hermeneutics, and Empire," 339.
37. Mahmood, "Secularism, Hermeneutics, and Empire," 339.
38. Mahmood, "Secularism, Hermeneutics, and Empire," 339–40.

While Mahmood seeks refuge in the immutable "metaphysical intentions" of the revealed text, she shows little awareness that such intentions—one can only surmise what she actually means by this—of any text is always subject to the divination of its intentions, meanings, and practices, which is the stock-in-trade of Muslim theologians. Legions of Muslim exegetes throughout history have read the Qur'ān as a book of signs and symbols without ever imagining that interpreting and resituating the text impugns its divine origins and inspiration. In fact, the Qur'ān proudly announces itself as a book of signs, consisting of multiple layers of meanings only available to earnest and committed readers. One would have to ascribe it to a monumental pratfall on Mahmood's part when she suggests that a "resituated" text is bereft of transcendence and loses a communitarian sensibility as if the private and public worlds were absolutely separated from one another. A glance at the Muslim hermeneutical tradition would reveal otherwise and would have prevented her from bowdlerizing a respectable tradition in her pious fury directed against Western secularism.

Figures such as Mahmood who oppose rethinking Muslim thought frequently offer no alternatives for faith communities trapped in narrow, suffocating, and anachronistic practices that do not resonate with their lived experiences. Such scholarly offerings, to my mind, often unwittingly reinforce practices and teachings that demean human dignity by shrill indictments of activists and scholars who strive to arrive at Islamic teachings that are consistent with Islam's broader ethical imperatives while maintaining strong faith commitments.[39] Some critics of "Islamic reform" find interpretive struggles as useful foils to prosecute meta-debates involving anti-liberal and anti-secular political struggles in which Islam and Muslims are merely ciphers. These battles occur at a distance from the daily struggles of ordinary Muslims who suffer large and small humiliations in their day-to-day religious practices under establishment Muslim political and religious authorities, whether they live under secular political regimes or under theocracies such as Iran and religiously-inspired monarchies like Saudi Arabia and several other Gulf states. Apart from the widely-noted suffering of Muslim women, which should not be politicized or demeaned by patriarchal interpretations of Muslim morality, numerous other issues merit more attention. Alas, this is hard to provide due to fears of scrutiny and disapproval offered by the likes of Iran's ayatollahs, the establishment clerics of al-Azhar in Cairo, or the Salafi ideologues of Saudi Arabia.

39. See Terman, "Islamophobia, Feminism, and the Politics of Critique."

These other issues would include interpretations by a range of Muslim orthodox actors who condone slavery and other anachronistic practices. Or, for instance, take damage done to free speech and human rights by condemnations of blasphemy justified under Sharīʿa governance. For critical traditionalist Muslims trying to live in a globalizing world by the lights of their faith and intellect, these issues present real dilemmas of conscience; they find themselves in a liminal space, sandwiched between powerful globalizing discourses of liberalism and secularism (both of which are not unfree from their own violence) on the one hand and cruelties done in the name of Muslim orthodoxies on the other.

But perhaps this liminal space is precisely where one ought to be in order to face the challenges and struggles of the future. The Marxist thinker Antonio Gramsci fully understood that the intellect allowed for a certain kind of pessimism to set in when one ponders the enormity of any major undertaking. But Gramsci also grasped that the reach of the human will could overcome this pessimism. Hence, he turned the French novelist Romain Rolland's maxim "pessimism of the intelligence, optimism of the will" into a guiding axiom for himself.[40] Yet Gramsci also had little patience with indifference and hence he fostered a life of activism. Reform-minded Muslims might heed Gramsci's words, embrace their liminality, and not remain on the sidelines.

Writing about tradition, Sherman A. Jackson engages the work of the Ghanaian scholar Kwame Geykye and provides illuminating insights. Tradition is not only about preservation, notes Jackson, but also about the role that the receiving generation or the "custodial generation" must play. "Tradition," Jackson writes, "is *not* the result of the simple *act* of transmission or handing down but of a *process* of evaluation, amplification, suppression, refinement, and assessing the polarity between would-be tradition and contemporary, indigenous innovations or nonindigenous ideas and practices." He then adds: "As long as no essential elements are deemed to have been sacrificed in this process of reception, the result will be a tradition that while only a simulacrum of the original is vested with all the authority of having resulted from a direct act of handing down."[41]

Debates over tradition in Islam today can be enriched by looking at how Muslim thinkers in the past dealt with "thought-styles" and practices around similar debates. I borrow the notion of "thought-style" (*Denkstil*)

---

40. Gramsci, *Selections from the Prison Notebooks*, 175.

41. Jackson, *Islam and the Problem of Black Suffering*, 42.

from the physician and scholar Ludwik Fleck (1896–1961), who examined how ideas emerge in complex scientific contexts, especially in the molecular field. Scientific facts, in his view, like any other facts (whether social or cultural), do not exist prior to an external world. But nor are they wholly determined features of the external world. Rather, scientific facts, like other modes of data, are "event[s] in the history of thought."[42] When people articulate those "events," they deploy certain social-psychological dispositions and operations for successful expression. Giving attention to these composites of social and psychic operations both enable and constrain the expression of complex ideas in what, again, Fleck calls "thought styles."[43] In many ways, traditions, too, are "thought styles" writ large, each having its own unique social-psychological features from which one might learn. To introduce a helpful thought-style, permit me now to examine how a towering scholar and intellectual from the Muslim past dealt with questions concerning tradition—in this case, with respect to medicine and faith healing.

IBN KHALDŪN EXAMINES ARGUMENTS FROM TRADITION

Few writers can be as thought-provoking as the late-medieval North African thinker ʿAbd al-Raḥmān Ibn Khaldūn (732–808 AH/1332–1406 CE) on virtually any topic, but especially in matters concerning tradition, a topic that surfaces repeatedly in his thought.

An intriguing and instructive argument emerges when Ibn Khaldūn compares two types of medical practices and remedies afoot during his day. One was the cosmopolitan and urban medicine of the cities, the other consisted of rural folk therapies. Medical practices dating back to the insights of the physician Galen were taken up later by Muslim admirers such as Abū Bakr al-Rāzī (d. c. 925–935), Abū al-Ḥasan al-Majūsī (d. 994), and Abū ʿAlī Ibn Sīna (d. 1037). Reflecting on their accomplishments, Ibn Khaldūn lamented the decline in the practice of medicine during his own time.[44] As a sub-discipline of physics (ṭabīʿyāt), Galenic medicine followed certain verifiable procedures and had certain well-defined features, among which was the well-known theory of balancing the bodily humors—namely blood, yellow bile, black bile, and phlegm. (Admittedly, Galenic medicine

42. Fleck, *Genesis and Development*.
43. Fleck, *Genesis and Development*.
44. Ibn Khaldūn, *Muqaddimah Ibn Khaldūn*, 479.

is not scientific in the modern sense, but it evinced a rigorous, "scientific" approach to natural phenomena.)

Rural medicine, by contrast, was based primarily on the experiences of a few elderly individuals, resulting in various folk remedies that were then handed down (*mutawārathan*) to subsequent generations. Such therapies from rural areas, to Ibn Khaldūn's mind, were not based on a clearly-defined science, but some folk remedies, he concedes, might be effective. Attempting to be even-handed, he explains how the apparent success of some of these remedies had produced well-known healers such as Ḥārith bin Kalada al-Thaqafī (d. 634–5) (known simply as Harth) from the city of Taif in the Arabian peninsula.

From Ibn Khaldūn's perspective, medical remedies transmitted (*manqūl*) over time and faithfully documented in the normative tradition (*shariʿyāt*) were matters of folk therapy and not based on science. Even though they were part of the canon of documented traditions and teachings (*ḥadīth* and *sunna*), he indicates that they should not be considered religiously normative and binding. In his view, their claims of therapy "have no grounding in revelation,"[45] but were "derived from what was customary (*ʿādiyan*) for the Arabs."[46] The only reason accounts of these remedies have come down to us, he insists, was due to the high value attached to the reported history of the lived circumstances (*aḥwāl*) of the Prophet Muhammad. One should keep in mind, Ibn Khaldūn continues, that the Prophet's medical practices derived from his particular cultural lifestyle, natural disposition, and preferences (*jibilla*) as a human being. These actions of the Prophet were "not derived from the perspective that it is a prescribed practice [of remedies] in a specified manner."[47] Averting the desire to give the Prophet's medicinal therapies a semi-sacred status, Ibn Khaldūn categorically states: "For surely the Prophet, on whom be peace and blessings, was commissioned to teach us the normative teachings (*sharāʾiʿ*)[48] and he *was not dispatched to instruct us in medicine and other customary matters.*"[49]

---

45. Ibn Khaldūn, *Muqaddimah Ibn Khaldūn*, 479.

46. Ibn Khaldūn, *Muqaddimah Ibn Khaldūn*, 479.

47. Ibn Khaldūn, *Muqaddimah Ibn Khaldūn*, 480.

48. I will explain later that *sharāʾiʿ* are normative instructions that are blended with teachings derived from revelation and prophetic utterances, but are also constituted by human labor and endeavors in the search for the good.

49. Ibn Khaldūn, *Muqaddimah Ibn Khaldūn*, 480 (emphasis added).

Readers might by now see where Ibn Khaldūn is heading. He wants to show that some practices and behaviors of the Prophet stemmed from the realm of the mundane and quotidian and should not enjoy normative status. But it is likely that some people conferred normative status on these practices, and so the topic was contested, as were many other topics, then and now.

To make his case, Ibn Khaldūn mentions two well-known incidents reported in the authoritative collections of prophetic reports and acknowledged by a large cross-section of Muslim sects and schools. Each example not only nuances the meaning of these reports but also allows one to derive certain analytic categories relevant for my own discussion of tradition, so permit them to be discussed in some detail. Ibn Khaldūn especially helps us steer through traditions and practices where the invocation of prophetic and divine authority might on the face of it sound daunting to challenge. Yet he weighs and evaluates these reports with the help of more capacious and historically-informed analytic categories in order to produce more compelling interpretive outcomes.

The first example concerns the Prophet Muhammad's disapproval of agricultural practices involving the cross-pollination of date-palm seedlings. When his companions stopped the practice in an effort to comply with his wishes, there followed a failed harvest of their staple. The Prophet in turn rebuked them in a statement that could apply to many quotidian matters: "You all [moreso then me] are more knowledgeable in matters related to your [agricultural] world."[50] In the remainder of the report, the Prophet added that his followers were only obliged to follow his commands in matters related to salvation practices (*dīn*) or what we today would call religious and moral matters. The implication of course is that in religious matters the Prophet speaks authoritatively, but in other matters he does not. The Prophet's admonition lends support to Ibn Khaldūn's reasoning that the Prophet was not sent as a medical expert or farming specialist. Ibn Khaldūn goes on to say that concerning these quotidian matters and in analogous ones reported in the authoritative manuals of Islamic civilization, they cannot be considered "prescriptive or normative" (*mashrū'*) since they do not contain compelling internal proof to raise them to such a level.[51]

The Prophet Muhammad's insistence that a man drink honey as a therapy for his afflicted stomach is my second example discussed by Ibn

50. Ibn Khaldūn, *Muqaddimah Ibn Khaldūn*, 480.
51. Ibn Khaldūn, *Muqaddimah Ibn Khaldūn*, 480.

Khaldūn. The Prophet in this instance invokes the truth of God and Scripture when a honey potion does not provide relief after two doses. The challenge that this episode poses for Ibn Khaldūn is complex and his solution should not be lost on jurists and theologians, who have the responsibility of determining what is truly sacred and what is not. What is at stake is this: if this teaching was seen as a religiously-normative precedent, it could impact and restrict how one views medicine and healing. Permit me, then, to develop the story since it crucially supports my argument about the difference between customary practices and "thought styles" on the one hand and the truly normative on the other—yet, I admit, the two are not altogether unrelated.

A man, the account goes, had a serious stomach ailment, and his brother became quite worried about him. Believing in the Prophet's charismatic healing power, the brother asked the Prophet to prescribe a remedy. The Prophet obliged and told the man to drink honey.

Honey is greatly esteemed by Muslims since many see its virtues through the lens of a parable in the Qur'ān 16:68–69, in which the exemplary humility, labor, and productivity of the bee are poetically described. The parable celebrates the production of a "drink of various colors" (presumably honey) and then follows with this line: "In *it* is a remedy for humanity." This line has given interpreters sufficient reason to associate honey with extraordinary health properties. But it is also possible to hold that the expression "*in it*" refers to the entire parable, not simply to the honey. (In my view, the parable's message is captured in: "Surely in *that* is a sign for people who reflect" [Q 16:69]. But this is not the focus of the interpreters and scholars under review.)

When the sick man's stomach failed to find relief after drinking honey as prescribed, the Prophet insists that he drink honey again. When the Prophet was told that the afflicted man's stomach still failed to heal, he addressed the man's petitioning brother in this revealing statement: "God spoke the truth and your brother's stomach is untruthful, make him drink honey."[52] After drinking honey for the third time, the man was reported to be relieved of his illness. And it appears that God's truth is a reference to the healing power of honey as confirmed in revelation.

Ibn Khaldūn does not linger on the story, but he finds a way of placing or "resituating" its contents to arrive at an interpretation within a larger,

---

52. Ibn Ḥajar al-ʿAsqalānī et al., *Fatḥ al-bārī*, 11:6837; *Ḥadīth* 5684 (*Kitāb al-Ṭibb*); Majlisī, *Biḥār*.

more compelling framework. We have already noted that he acknowledged both the validity of natural science-based Galenic medicine and folk remedies. If believers used folk remedies as an act of spirituality or to affirm solidarity with the Prophet, Ibn Khaldūn concedes that surely blessings will follow. Such remedies in fact are intricately connected to affective realities, religious liturgy, belief in faith healing, and spirituality.[53] They draw on the presence of the supernatural, Ibn Khaldūn says, and depend on the "formulaic traditions of faith-infused words" (āthār al-kalimāt al-īmānīya). The Prophet's recommendation of medicinal honey is on par with the use of formulaic words of faith for healing. But Ibn Khaldūn just as clearly maintains that such pious actions not be mistaken for actual science, for which he also has high regard.

Ibn Khaldūn's elegant resolution of the matter requires an interpretation (hermeneutic) on his part to resituate past practices within a plausible historical framework. In this instance, his task was relatively easy. He identified natural science-based medicine as discursively intelligible and as a historically established genre bearing its own rationales. By contrast, folkloric and rural medicine were in the realm of the local and were inflected with liturgical faith-healing properties and performances. Once he could identify two different types of healing practices, his task to provide reasonable explanations for each from the past became plausible, if not absolutely convincing.

More broadly, Ibn Khaldūn provides a crucial insight about how creatively and incisively tradition could be dealt with in the premodern world. One must approach tradition with the scalpel of a surgeon, he seems to say, together with a nuanced skepticism. Doing so provides one with the ability to discern different logics of practice at work by means of "radical contextualization."[54] Ibn Khaldūn could have easily acquiesced to the authority of tradition and accepted honey simply as a wonder potion. Recall how the Prophet's intimidating rhetoric seemed to pit the truth of God's revealed speech about the remedial powers of honey against the "untruthful" stomach of the sick man. Yet Ibn Khaldūn remained undaunted by the face value of the Prophet's rhetoric since he possessed "an eminent heuristic virtue"[55] and had the capacity to enter the fields of history, culture, sci-

---

53. He explains how this healing works is: "'alā jiha-t al-tabarruk wa ṣidq al-'aqd al-īmānī—from the perspective of spiritual blessing and an affirmation of a commitment to faith" (Ibn Khaldūn, Muqaddimah Ibn Khaldūn, 480).

54. Bourdieu, Field of Cultural Production, 9.

55. Bourdieu, Field of Cultural Production, 29.

ence, and juridical hermeneutics of "relational thinking"[56] simultaneously. Deploying his knowledge and skills, Ibn Khaldūn both empathizes with the sincere piety behind folk healing practices while maintaining that they still do not add up to actual science. In short, he makes a distinction crucial for religious hermeneutics.

Finally, it is interesting to note that the Cairo-based expert on prophetic traditions, Ibn Ḥajar al-ʿAsqalānī (d.1449), who lived roughly two centuries before Ibn Khaldūn, provides copious reference to authors who wrote about the medicinal properties of honey in his commentary of prophetic reports. ʿAsqalānī's authorities also report that honey does not serve as a blanket remedy for all illnesses and all persons.[57] ʿAsqalānī reports the majority of scholars saying that the referent "in *it* is a remedy for humanity" refers to honey. However, ʿAsqalānī claims that many exegetes of the Qurʾān think the possessive pronoun "it" in fact refers to the Qurʾān as a whole, as a spiritual remedy for humanity.[58] In other words, the signs and words of the Qurʾān are the remedial honey. A later expert of traditions, Bāqir al-Majlisī (d.1110/1698), three centuries after Ibn Khaldūn, argues that it is grammatically incoherent for the referent to mean the Qurʾān. Still, he affirms earlier authorities who claim that honey can be medicinal, but it can also harm someone suffering from bile.[59] In Majlisī's view, the messenger of God persisted in his prescription of honey for the sick man on the grounds that divinely inspired knowledge and intuitions—his "light of revelation" (*nūr al-waḥī*), vouchsafed to Muhammad alone—assured him in this particular case, but not necessarily in all others, that honey could be an effective remedy.[60]

To return to Ibn Khaldūn, one senses that he is generally agnostic about supernatural powers and feats if they are not explicitly corroborated by authoritative teachings in either the Qurʾān or in sound reports from the Prophet. He is inclined to dismiss messiahs and millenarian figures, even if he admits supernatural realities and believes that they can even be the subject of discursive understanding. In the final analysis, the Prophet's cure of the man with a stomach ailment appears plausible to Ibn Khaldūn. But since he sees this as an extremely rare, supernatural event, the method

56. Bourdieu, *Field of Cultural Production*, 29.
57. Ibn Ḥajar al-ʿAsqalānī et al., *Fatḥ al-bārī*, 11:6837.
58. Ibn Ḥajar al-ʿAsqalānī et al., *Fatḥ al-bārī*, 11:6837.
59. Majlisī, *Biḥār*, 61:233.
60. Majlisī, *Biḥār*, 61:233.

of the cure might only apply in this specific instance and should not be mistaken for precedent-setting medical advice.

CONCLUSION

Understanding debates about the place of tradition in Islam—and perhaps seeing these as a resource for other faith traditions—requires a familiarity with the complexity of the Muslim tradition, past and present, and a recognition of just how contested engagement with tradition has become in our own day and age among Muslims. At least this much is true at the scholarly level with respect to the interpretation of sacred texts and their meaning and implications today. At a more popular level, even without such scholarly analysis, Muslims across the globe remain deeply engaged in a variety of tradition-based practices that reflect the beauty, intricacy, and diversity of Islam.

I hope this chapter has shown how Azmeh and Jad'an and other scholars have proposed nuanced and creative ways to help one conceptually and practically engage with tradition—ways that require careful reading and interpretation and a keen sense of history and its impact on lived societies. By contrast, I hope to have pointed out how Saba Mahmood instrumentalized tradition as a weapon against liberalism and secularism; she reduced tradition to the singular, if not the absolute, by failing to carefully engage in the deeper resources of Islamic thought.

Ibn Khaldūn, moreover, shows us that tradition can be quite complex and to understand it, one must grapple with this complexity. He managed to craft two kinds of moral or spiritual economies at work in his account of different types of medicine advocated by tradition: the economy of the art or science of medicine on one hand and the charismatic economy of the social miracle of prophetic medicine and folk therapies on the other. Both have validity *as tradition*, but only once the proper hermeneutic is deployed to distinguish between them.

The interpretative questions facing Islam today are in many respects not dissimilar to those faced by Ibn Khaldūn. Some advocates of Muslim tradition steer people in the direction of that which is affirmed as permanent and persistent (*thābit*, pl. *thawābit*). They even want to expand the domain of what is resolutely permanent. By contrast, others raise questions about this direction and appear to want to deny that tradition possesses absolute permanence. The former frequently charge the latter of denying the tradition, while the latter charge the former with the unwarranted absolutizing of tradition.

The tension between these competing directions raise acute questions about what I will call moral ontology. Would moving against that which is perceived to be the permanent in tradition-based practices be tantamount to a negation of moral ontology? In my view it would not. It would, however, introduce greater pluralism, nuance, and latitude into how one interprets and practices a tradition; it would expand one's moral-ontological horizon, as it were, in conversation with the present. And this expansion can even be a good and necessary thing, even if at first it might appear inadmissibly altering or reassigning the valuation of the permanent. But under these changed conditions, the permanent gains a different, broader horizon in which to realize itself. In fact, as the moral-ontological horizon shifts, what was once deemed as permanent and persistent in the tradition does not disappear altogether. Far from it. It is simply recoded and rethought, as one applies the tradition's first principles to new circumstances and new knowledge, often even while drawing from the past, as I have drawn in this chapter from Ibn Khaldūn.

Thus understood, and returning to a previous biological analogy, tradition always has a "metabolic" character; it continuously remakes and refines itself, blending old and new, past and present, changing but remaining permanent nonetheless.

5

Tradition

A Lutheran Perspective

Sarah Hinlicky Wilson
Lutheran Forum

TRADITION IS THE ABILITY to think. Tradition takes a human mind, which can be formed in any of countless directions, and assembles the data of the world, which can be selected and arranged in any of countless ways, connecting mind and data by means of a coherent starting point and a trajectory. Tradition is the opposite of randomness and meaningless: it is coherence and sense.

Of course, because there are so many minds and so much data, there are also many traditions. And each of these many traditions is extended in its encounter with more minds and more data, which means that none of them is static, even if some remain identifiably the same over long periods of time. Furthermore, traditions encounter each other and have to cope with the challenge of other thought patterns, which may well call into question their own. But all of this is a matter of ongoing human thinking, thinking well, thinking deeply.

And that is all I have to say in defense of tradition in general. I consider the many fashionable arguments against tradition to be void of sense: they are, after all, their own traditions of thought, many of them shockingly shallow. What interests me far more, as an avowed partisan of the Lutheran theological tradition who remains nevertheless committed to the encounter with other theological and religious traditions, is the challenge of the ongoing life of my tradition.[1] I expect all partisans of a tradition feel the same concern. So in this essay I will take up three problems any religious tradition might face from the perspective of my own; and, to practice what I preach, I will draw on episodes in my tradition in order to unearth strategies to help. The first focuses on the movement of a tradition across cultural and national boundaries and how thinkers within a tradition evaluate adaptations and additions in light of the threat of syncretic and possibly fatal compromises—in this case, I will look briefly at Africa before focusing on early Lutheran missions in India. The second problem is the challenge a tradition faces when altogether new questions arise—in this instance, that of women's public discourse in the church. The final section tackles the difficulty of recognizing an irredeemable aspect of a tradition—in this case, Christian anti-Judaism. In each case, but especially in the latter two, I am interested in how practitioners draw from resources within their tradition to mitigate or excise other elements in the same tradition. Finally, I should note that I am especially interested in missiological questions: how do we communicate our traditions in such a way that we invite new persons into them—or perhaps reinvite estranged persons back into them—so these people can both receive from our traditions and also contribute to them?

---

1. This approach to tradition from a Lutheran may well run counter to generic stereotypes about Lutheranism or Protestantism more generally. Besides the obvious fact that my specific Christian tradition is now half a millennium old and builds on a Christian tradition that existed three times longer beforehand, which itself is built on the still older Jewish tradition, I may point to the important work of, among others in the twentieth century, Jaroslav Pelikan, who played a key role in altering Lutherans' often misleading self-perception of being based purely on the Bible without acknowledging our deep formation in Reformation-era and other Christian texts and practices. This book has already been mentioned by others, but see especially Pelikan, *Vindication of Tradition*, which trades somewhat on the supposed anti-tradition stance of Luther and Lutherans in order to dispel it.

EXTENDING THE TRADITION TO NEW PLACES AND CULTURES

Although we probably underestimate the degree to which peoples in the past were aware of the cultural and religious "other," it certainly is true that awareness of human diversity has grown at an extraordinary speed in the past several centuries, and its pace only increases. This has never been an easy thing to accept—we are all naturally biased in favor of our own ways of being in human community—and a response of scorn and violence is as evident now as ever. But one distinct aspect of our accelerating (late) modernity is responding to this human diversity with a kind of shrugged-shoulders relativism. People like what they like; there are no universal standards; your way is as good as mine as long as you don't force it on me, et cetera, et cetera. There is much to be said politically for such a hands-off approach, but human souls and communities do not flourish if they believe that everything about them is purely arbitrary and unnecessary.

One way to protect a tradition from the emptiness of relativism is to circle the wagons and batten down the hatches. Such may be necessary in certain cases for pure survival—say, in situations of persecution—but this is not a good strategy overall: it leads to stagnation and, more often than not, a great deal of defection when the tradition refuses to account for the wider world. A more fruitful way forward is to foster and learn from the cross-cultural reception of the tradition.

A brief example will illustrate the point. Norwegian Pietism is for all intents and purposes dead in Norway and nearly dead among the Norwegian-American immigrant communities in the United States; it has ceased to speak to the people of these societies. But there is one place where it is alive and well: Madagascar. The Malagasy Lutheran Church is a thriving concern where Pietism lives on, though of course much transformed. The centerpiece of its ministry is exorcism, addressing the local concern with possession by evil spirits, witchcraft, and an indigenous religion strongly oriented toward the dead. In fact, the indigenous music of Madagascar is so tied up with the indigenous religion that Malagasy Christians have not adapted it for use in hymnody: it can't yet be disentangled from the old evil ways. The Lutherans there sing rather dreary Pietist hymns in the Norwegian musical style before commanding the demons to depart in Jesus' name.[2] But it is not the same to the northwest, across the Mozambique

---

2. See the discussion in Vigen, "Missions, Revivals, and Diakonia."

Channel in Tanzania, where local Christians have perceived a more positive continuity between their indigenous worship of the Creator and the message that the missionaries brought to them concerning Jesus the redeemer and the Holy Spirit. Christianity added to a pre-existent Creator: faith, the cross, the forgiveness of sins, and everlasting life. The continuity in this case was strong enough for Tanzanian Lutherans to politely reject European church bells and summon their people to worship with their indigenous drums instead—not a viable move for the Malagasy.[3] But either way, these two communities have received and interpreted the Christian tradition and are the fastest-growing Lutheran churches in the world today (outstripped possibly only by Ethiopia's Lutheran church).

To explore a tradition's cross-cultural transmission in more depth, permit me now to shift attention to India and look at two seminal figures there: the German missionary Bartholomäus Ziegenbalg (1682–1719) and the Tamil Indian teacher and poet Vedanayagam Sastriar (1774–1864).

Ziegenbalg was twenty-three years old when he landed at the south Indian fortress of Tranquebar on July 9, 1706. The governor of this Danish colony refused to let him disembark for three days because his intention to share the gospel with the locals would interfere with the Danish East India Company's habits of drinking, womanizing, and slaveholding. Exiled to the "bad" part of town, namely among the indigenous Tamils, Ziegenbalg found an elderly blind man who instructed Tamil youth in their language. He squatted down on the floor with the children and learned to write the letters in the sand just as they did. Blessed with a prodigious memory, Ziegenbalg read and reread Tamil palm-leaf manuscripts up to a hundred times until he had mastered them. Within eight months, Ziegenbalg was speaking Tamil and translating works into Tamil, such as—no surprise—the Bible and Luther's Small Catechism.

Tamil was not an easy language to master. It had both a poetic and a colloquial form, and the latter had not yet been codified in writing. Recognizing a need, Ziegenbalg gave Tamils their colloquial language in written form, which is in use to this day, and in 1716 he published his *Grammatica Damulica*, the first Tamil grammar to use Tamil characters. He also recognized the local importance of Portuguese, the language of the Jesuit Catholics who had settled in Tranquebar earlier, so he put his mind to that task as well and soon was producing Portuguese translations.

---

3. As exemplified in the case of Josiah Kibira (1925–1988), bishop in Tanzania and president of the Lutheran World Federation. See Larson, *Bishop Josiah Kibira*, 22–23.

He also translated a number of Tamil works into German, as impressed by their ethical sophistication as he was horrified by their polytheism.

In due course Ziegenbalg built a church for Tamil converts (the Europeans who even bothered to go to church refused to admit them) and set up schools for both boys and girls, making him the founder of female education in South India. But the local governor of the colony would have none of it and threw Ziegenbalg in jail on the grounds that he was "the servant of the devil." After a month in a state of shock from his solitary confinement, Ziegenbalg recovered when friends smuggled him pen and paper, and he spent the rest of his four-month sentence writing a pair of devotional manuals.

Things got better after that, for awhile, anyway. A new missionary colleague named Johann Ernst Gründler arrived, and between the two of them, they translated all of the New Testament into Tamil. They found support from Anglicans in Madras and Armenian Orthodox businessmen—a real blessing because the Danish king got himself involved in a protracted war with Sweden and stopped sending money. Ziegenbalg and Gründler established a seminary, and the first Indian Lutheran pastor, Aaron, was ordained in 1733.

Tragically, for all the resistance Ziegenbalg encountered from the colonial authorities, the opposition that really did him in came from one of his own. The new director of the Danish Mission Board, Christian Wendt, had no firsthand experience of mission work or cross-cultural encounter: all he knew was that he despised everything Ziegenbalg and Gründler were doing. Wendt thought missionaries should simply preach and move on. Accordingly, he cut off their funding for church buildings, schools, orphanages, hospitals, and printing presses. Wendt had no understanding of the social cost to Tamils of turning their backs on caste and family or the need of the church to provide them with a new family and a new vocation along with their new faith. Wendt's mission to destroy Ziegenbalg's reputation was so effective that the poor man, never of a strong constitution, succumbed and died after a long illness in 1719.

As disturbing as Wendt's campaign was, against missionaries and Tamils alike, even Ziegenbalg hadn't arrived in India already knowing how to relate to people so culturally and religiously different from himself. He admitted, "Before I lived among them, I, too, had similar prejudices. Nevertheless, after I learned to speak the Tamil language, at least to some extent, and to discuss with them all kinds of things, I gradually gave up my wrong ideas. I learned to understand the people better. Finally, when I read their books, I realized that they have an orderly way of teaching complex philosophical doctrines and other disciplines."[4]

The result was that he did not condemn everything about the Indian way of life. Quite the contrary: he found much to admire. Spiritual ignorance, *akkiyānam* in Tamil, was not something unique to India but rather afflicted people in every corner of the world—including "Christian" Europe. When Ziegenbalg engaged locals in dialogue, whether they were Hindus following *bhakti* devotional practices or Muslims of the Sufi strain, he assumed that they already knew something true about God and moral action.

He recorded, for example, a dialogue between himself and a Brahmin. The two men agreed that there is only one God, but the Brahmin claimed that from this one God, many other deities have emanated, including evil ones. Ziegenbalg challenged the Brahmin on this point: how could he believe something as contradictory as God setting fire to his own residence by introducing evil to a good creation? The Brahmin responded, "Our religion is the oldest on earth; many pious kings followed it. Several sages followed it. So I also follow it." Ziegenbalg retorted: "Antiquity of a thing cannot prove its true nature because Satan and sin are also old."[5] A salutary warning for those inclined to equate the value of a tradition with its age!

But the larger point is Ziegenbalg's willingness to see the good in Tamil religious tradition, even to admire the devotion in it. He worked with it, not against it, to expand its range, introducing new vocabulary to describe the hitherto not-fully-known God: *Caruvecuran* for "the Supreme God," *Tirittuvam* to qualify God as "triune," and *Naracīvatayāparar* to describe God as "the One who is merciful toward all living things." He wrote a moral treatise called *The Way of Dharma*, translated the Danish liturgy into Tamil, and freely borrowed Jesuit translations of Christian terms, like *Narkarunai*, literally "good grace," for holy communion.

Ziegenbalg's mission method was unprecedented in the Lutheran tradition. Indeed, it was inconceivable to most Lutherans back in Europe. They could not fathom how one would go about introducing the gospel to a place that had not heard it, excusing their apathy on the grounds that the apostles had already taken the gospel everywhere God intended it to go. The bishop of Denmark initially refused to ordain Ziegenbalg because

4. Ziegenbalg quoted in Jeyaraj, *Bartholomäus Ziegenbalg*, 125.
5. Ziegenbalg quoted in Jeyaraj, *Bartholomäus Ziegenbalg*, 126.

there was no pre-existing congregation to which he could be ordained. And yet the results of this cross-cultural communication of the Christian tradition were enormously fruitful. Ziegenbalg became not only the first Protestant missionary in India but is also said to be the first European Indologist, pioneering the study of other religions as an academic discipline.[6]

Ziegenbalg brought the gospel message from without; swiftly, though, there were Indians who took it up from within. Less than a century after Ziegenbalg's mission, Vedanayagam Sastriar took the inculturation of the gospel into Tamil forms even further. Although he had been educated by Western missionaries, his keenest interest lay in the indigenous Tamil forms of poetry and literature, despite the fact that their content was entirely concerned with Hindu beliefs and piety.

Like the Tanzanians with their drums, Vedanayagam perceived no fundamental opposition between the gospel and local artistic expression. At the age of sixteen, he began evangelizing in rural areas by means of traditional songs set with gospel-infused words, and his works only grew in sophistication from there. From the text of the Song of Songs he crafted an *antati*—a bhakti poem in which "the last words or their rhymes are the first words of the next stanza, and the last stanza ends the way the first begins to form an unbroken verbal garland of sound."[7] Later, he did another version of the Song of Songs in *kummi* form, circle dancing with clapping that was used during religious festivals.

Yet another indigenous form, the *Kuravañci* or dramatic dance, was adapted by Vedanayagam to become "The Fortune Teller's Dance-Drama of the Lord of Bethlehem," a direct rival to a local dance drama about the Hindu god Shiva. On preaching tours, he used the form known as *Kālatcēpam*, alternating homilies with song accompanied by a band. Vedanayagam also composed countless hymns over the course of forty-five years, setting them to the south Indian devotional music traditions. He even used the Sanskrit devotional word *Ōm* to translate the Greek *Logos*: "In the beginning was the *Ōm*"—a risk that quite a few missionaries found too risky.

His lifetime's work of translating the gospel not only linguistically but also culturally and artistically earned Vedanayagam many accolades in a culture that loved to adorn its leaders with lavish titles, including "Grand

---

6. In addition to Jeyaraj's thorough and excellent study, see Gilbert, "Archived Wisdom," as well as Gilbert's excellent documentary on Ziegenbalg, *Beyond Empires*. See also Kolb, "Three-Hundredth Anniversary"; Scherer, "Bartholomew Ziegenbalg."

7. Hudson, *Protestant Origins in India*, 118.

Master of Scripture and Poems of Superior Wisdom," "The Emperor among Evangelical Bards," "Royal Bard Who Is the Light of Wisdom," and "Scholar of Scripture." Vedanayagam even received the red hat conferred on Muslim teachers by the local Muslim ruler, the Nawab of Arcot, in recognition of his wisdom. He wore it for the rest of his life.[8]

As we can see from the cases of these two Christians in India, tradition lives not only by its transmission through the generations but also in its transmission to new places and cultures. Both Ziegenbalg and Vedanayagam were handing on what had been handed to them by a long chain of apostles—the good news about Jesus Christ. But at the same moment, they were also doing things unknown to their traditions before: Ziegenbalg pushing the Lutheran commitment to the vernacular beyond its usual comfortable limits, Vedanayagam investing traditional Tamil Hindu forms with entirely new content. In so doing, they passed on the tradition, but they also added to it and gave it new life. As the Christian faith continues to live and grow in India, it is a matter of ongoing testing to determine to what extent these adaptations are faithful or not and whether they require still more adaptation. It is also a live question whether the peoples and cultures of the West who passed the tradition on to Indian Christians will today be able to receive back what the Indian Christians have added to it and so experience for themselves new life in the tradition. This is a question much larger than the Lutheran-Indian example given here but relevant to many "Global-South" locations in their relations with their more secularized, erstwhile colonial masters.

POSING A NEW QUESTION TO THE TRADITION

My examples from Africa and India point to the challenge of maintaining a tradition across space—across cultural and national boundaries. Another challenge is maintaining a tradition across time—through the course of human history, with all its developments and changes. Through time, traditions find that they must face new questions. It is to this challenge that I now turn, taking questions about women's public discourse in the church as my primary example.

An illuminating case of the fate of women in Christian tradition is the changing translation of Romans 16:7. In this last chapter of the epistle, Paul greets a number of folks in Rome, and among them his "relatives who were

8. Vethanayagamony, "St. Vedanayagam Sastriar," 36–40.

in prison" with him, two people who are "prominent among the apostles" and "in Christ before" he was, namely Andronicus and—well—somebody. The latter figure used to be called Junia: thus the King James Version and every other English translation up to the 1830s. But no small number of English translations since then have identified this person as Junias, with the -s on the end, rendering the figure a man rather than a woman.

This is a wonderful example of the intricate ironies inherent to a tradition. Every church father, without exception, took Andronicus's coworker to be Junia, a woman. Even John Chrysostom, not exactly known for his positive thoughts about the female sex, commented, "How great the wisdom of this woman must have been that she was even deemed worthy of the title of apostle." Yet a millennium and a half later, scholars concluded *not* that her wisdom was so great but rather that if she was worthy of the title "apostle," then she wasn't a *she* at all.

Historical-critical study found the leadership of a woman unthinkable and so made Junia into Junias, a male name, even though there is not a single record of the name Junias anywhere in ancient Rome. Extraordinary feats of scholarly gymnastics concocted reasons for the sex-change operation—ignoring not only the textual and archaeological evidence to the contrary but also the contextual fact that Paul himself had no difficulty in assigning evangelical prominence to women: entrusting the epistle to deaconess Phoebe and identifying seven of the women in his greetings as contributing the most to the churches, while only five men received that distinction. In verses 6 and 12 of Romans 16, four of the women are said to have "worked very hard," which is the same verbal construct Paul used to describe his own apostolic ministry in 1 Corinthians 4:12, Galatians 4:11, and Philippians 2:16.[9]

In short, modern scholarship had serious blinders on where Junia was concerned, as compared to earlier traditions of interpretation. Yet at the same time, traditional interpreters never perceived or felt a need to draw any further conclusions from the scriptural attestation to a female apostle. It would take nearly two millennia of sitting with such texts before widespread questions began to be raised within the church about the public role of women in the transmission of the Christian faith.

Even so, these questions are not entirely without precedent before the nineteenth century. Though public women in the church are few and far between, they do exist—from Monica and Macrina in the early church,

9. Epp, *Junia*.

to Hildegard of Bingen, Catherine of Siena, and Christine de Pisan in the Middle Ages, to a growing number from the sixteenth century onward. Inevitably, when they spoke about the faith, they also had to speak about the fact that they were speaking about the faith *as* women. The tradition of Christian women speaking was so modest that they rarely knew about each other and thus could not build on one another's resources. In a sense, Christian women had to reinvent the wheel every time, lacking a tradition of women's discourse that would direct their thinking and allow them to build on their predecessors. This brings into focus my second challenge in the transmission of tradition: namely, how to address a *new* question arising with the resources *already present* in the tradition, resources that have not yet been put to that particular use.

To explore this topic in greater length, I will turn now to an impressive woman of the Lutheran Reformation, Argula von Grumbach (1492–1568).[10] She was a noblewoman of the von Stauff line but held no authority in matters legal or juridical. She was literate but had received no formal education. She was a wife, a mother of four, and a busy household manager. And she was the only one in all of Ingolstadt (Bavaria) to come to the defense of one Arsacius Seehofer. He had arrived in town as a university tutor after a stint studying in Wittenberg, where he learned Lutheran teachings such as faith alone is sufficient for justification and that God imputes his own righteousness to us apart from our works. Word got around, and before long, Arsacius's rooms were searched, his possessions seized, and he was forced to recant before the entire university. No man came to Arsacius's defense; it was much too dangerous. But Argula did.

She had always been an avid reader. Early in life, she received an illustrated German Bible from her father (her brothers did not!); late in life, her correspondents gently chided her for failing to return borrowed books in a timely fashion. When Luther's writings were smuggled into Bavaria, she devoured them. Her brother had been present at Arsacius's show trial, and the proceedings so outraged her that, shortly thereafter, she wrote a public letter to the University of Ingolstadt defending Arsacius, Luther, and Melanchthon, challenging the professors to a public debate on the contested matters and altogether defying the ordinance against religious dissent in Bavaria.

10. A translation of all of Argula von Grumbach's known writings can be found in Matheson, *Argula von Grumbach*. See also Matheson's biography, *Argula von Grumbach (1492–1554/7)*.

Such a thing was unheard of—a woman interjecting herself into politics and religion alike. She was well aware of it. "I suppressed my inclinations," she wrote in her letter; "heavy of heart, I did nothing. Because Paul says in 1 Timothy 2: 'The women should keep silence and should not speak in church.' But now that I cannot see any man who is up to it, who is either willing or able to speak, I am constrained by the saying: 'Whoever confesses me,'"[11] in Matthew 10. She also cites Ezekiel 33, "If you see your brother sin, reprove him, or I will require blood at your hands." And Luke 9, "Whoever is ashamed of me and of my words, I too will be ashamed of when I come in my majesty," on which she comments: "Words like these, coming from the very mouth of God, are always before my eyes. For they exclude neither woman nor man."[12]

In these citations she lays her finger on the difficulty: there is a tension in the scriptural witness regarding a woman's public voice. One strain seems to require her silence, another seems to require her speech. How, then, to adjudicate between the two? In Argula's judgment, when such matters as the gospel are at stake, the command to speak makes a greater claim than the command to be silent. As such, Matthew 10 became the charter of her Christian discipleship. Indeed, her very baptism obligated her to speak.

For further proof of the rightness of her speech, Argula appealed to the precedent set by St. Jerome, who, she observed, "was not ashamed of writing a great deal to women, to Blesilla, for example, to Paula, Eustochium and so on." And this, in turn, causes her to recall that "Christ himself, he who is the only teacher of us all, was not ashamed to preach to Mary Magdalene, and to the young woman at the well."[13] Note that in both these cases, women are the recipients of teaching rather than the sources of it—but Argula infers that those who are taught are invited to know, to speak, and even themselves to teach. You don't educate someone whom you expect to remain silent.

Argula's letter was an overnight bestseller, going through fourteen editions in the next two months. The Ingolstadt theologians were beside themselves. Of course, it was hardly to Argula's advantage that she was speaking in defense of the Lutheran heresy. But the accusations against her did not primarily refer to her theological outlook but rather to her sex. A local preacher, Georg Hauer, declaimed from the pulpit against the "wretched

11. Matheson, *Argula von Grumbach*, 79.

12. Matheson, *Argula von Grumbach*, 75.

13. Matheson, *Argula von Grumbach*, 88.

children of Eve" and leveled accusations against "you female desperado," "you wretched and pathetic daughter of Eve," "you arrogant devil," "you arrogant fool," "you heretical bitch," and "you shameless whore."[14] Chancellor Leonhard von Eck insisted that this "female devil" be punished.[15] He even accused her of the unthinkable: of having *preached* in Dietfurt! But since all she had done was write letters and, as a woman, she had no official power, the best he could do was to get her husband, Friedrich, dismissed from his post, throwing the family into a spiral of debt and litigation from which they never escaped. Some of the Bavarian authorities also suggested, none too subtly, that Friedrich ought to shut Argula up by any means necessary, and no one would blame him.

If the Ingolstadt theologians thought that such measures would silence Argula, they were profoundly mistaken. She went on to become one of the bestselling pamphleteers of the sixteenth century, with about 30,000 copies of her seven public writings ending up in print. She enjoyed great popular support. In April 1524 a satire of the Ingolstadt theologians circulated, depicting them as denouncing young Arsacius "for believing that lay people and women can be theologians, which is clearly impossible since only men can be ordained, and since all theologians are men." It was popularly believed that Argula was more educated than most churchmen and had committed the entire Bible to memory. A woodcut gracing a compilation of her writings shows Argula, Bible in hand, facing off with a whole court of university theologians, whose textbooks and *summae* have fallen to the ground as if dead. Argula herself believed that if her opponents inflicted martyrdom upon her, "a hundred women would emerge to write against them."[16] Being a woman or a layperson or even a duke was no excuse for being "as well informed about the Bible as a cow is about chess."[17] For "*all Christians* do have a responsibility to know the word of God."[18]

Notably, Argula's last publication was a poem, which was a response to another poem, entitled, "A Word about the Stauffen Woman and her Disputatiousness," a coarse, vulgar, and scurrilous attack on her character. Quoting no Scripture other than a few verses from 1 and 2 Timothy, the sole purpose of the poem's pseudonymous author was to discredit Argula

14. Matheson, *Argula von Grumbach*, 19.
15. Matheson, *Argula von Grumbach*, 18.
16. Matheson, *Argula von Grumbach*, 120.
17. Matheson, *Argula von Grumbach*, 146.
18. Matheson, *Argula von Grumbach*, 146 (emphasis added).

as a promiscuous wild animal who had brazenly abandoned her spindle and thread. Undaunted, she actually reprinted the original poem along with her own withering response, calling out the coward to meet her in public debate instead of hiding behind an assumed name. (He never did, and we still do not know the author.) Her poem assembled a much more impressive range of Scripture, too, from God speaking through Balaam's ass in Numbers 22, to the outpouring of the Holy Spirit on all flesh, male and female alike, in Joel 3, to the stories of biblical and apocryphal heroines, especially the warrior women Deborah, Jael, and Judith. By this time, her fame was so great that, when she traveled to the Diet of Augsburg in 1530, Emperor Charles V sent her a personal note warning her to keep quiet!

The terrible irony of Argula's story is that, once again, a flowering of women's discourse in the church was forgotten. She was remembered episodically but has only become a focus of renewed interest and research in the past two decades. What she came to understand about Christian women's speech had to be rediscovered and reinvented by later Christian women.

Needless to say, questions about women's public speech in the life of the church, and beyond that in their public authority and leadership, remain as relevant as ever. Though the reader can no doubt infer my position on these issues, my purpose here is not to attempt to solve the problem but to point out the specific challenge it poses to those of us who think from and with a tradition. There is simply precious little to go on. Certainly, there is more within Scripture on women than has received attention over the centuries, but it is not an overwhelming or unambiguous legacy; the same holds for much of church history. Attempts to resolve the question by appeal to the past, whether for or against, struggle with the thinness of the data. Even on that most neuralgic of issues, the ordination of women to ministry of the church, the sheer fact that it was not done is accompanied by virtual silence on why that should be the case. It seems that the question simply did not occur to previous generations. Was the non-ordination of women a tradition, an inertia, an oversight? Was it inherent to the gospel or a problem waiting to be addressed at a later point? With what resources do we assess the proposal now?[19]

The one thing clear is that it is not an option for traditions today to ignore the new questions—on women or any other new topic. Our traditions

---

19. As an example of this difficulty, see my discussion of the problem of the tradition's silence in Wilson, *Woman, Women, and the Priesthood,* 146–51.

must provide resources and freedom for addressing them or risk being sidelined, discredited, and forgotten.

EXCISING A DESTRUCTIVE ASPECT FROM THE TRADITION

My third example of a challenge to the ongoing life of a tradition is when those who live from the tradition recognize a strain within in it so bad, so irredeemable, that it has to be cut off once and for all. This is a threatening prospect on many levels. First, there is the obvious problem of the community agreeing that some aspect of the tradition is beyond redemption rather than just being obnoxious to our late and unredeemed biases and therefore still deserving of ongoing struggle. Second, even if we did agree on the irredeemability of some aspect of the tradition, we would have to pose the hard question of whether this aspect was inherently bound up with other vital aspects of the tradition—so entangled with one another that to jettison the irredeemable part might suggest abandoning the tradition entirely. I am sure we are all well aware of those who have left our traditions after coming to exactly this conclusion. But even supposing we concluded that the tradition could be salvaged once purified of the wicked strain within it, we would still be faced with the issue of how to go about the work of extracting it, how to deal with the collateral damage, and whether we could find positive resources from within the tradition to apply *against* the part we need to excise—tradition against tradition, as it were.

My case study here is Christian anti-Judaism. Growing up as I did on this side of the Shoah, I was always taught that hatred of the Jews, their "race" and their religion alike, was completely unacceptable from a Christian point of view. But of course, it takes very little study of Christian history to realize what a minority report that view is. If that view has become more widespread now (sadly, not yet universal), it is only because of how the terrible twentieth century forced a reckoning at unbearable cost.

Only recently, though, I have begun to see more clearly how deep the roots of Christian anti-Judaism go. By this I mean not so much the racial anti-Semitism that has dominated the last two centuries—though that is never very far away—but the habitual "dyadic" thinking (to use the Jewish theologian Peter Ochs's term) that is deeply ingrained in us, such that even the most self-styled liberal, progressive, inclusive Christians who otherwise noisily decry anti-Semitism thoughtlessly indulge in it. As an example, here is an excerpt from a sermon submitted to a competition on which I was a judge. I know nothing about the preacher except that he or she is a Lutheran pastor of my denomination and a graduate from one of our seminaries that would certainly rank itself in the "progressive" and "inclusive" camp. Allow me to quote:

> Christians . . . stand in the legacy of repeated cries for freedom. Almost two thousand years ago, St. Paul urged Gentile converts not to fall prey to those who would impose upon them the entire Mosaic law. . . . To force circumcision on the converts was to cut them off from the freedom of Christ and the hope of the Gospel. It was to make following Jesus something that was endured and earned, rather than freely given. To force circumcision saw Gentiles as children of the flesh, rather than children of the promise. . . . In most of our contexts at least, we can breathe a sigh of relief that the circumcision faction has died out.

It is easy to hear this as a standard exposition of Paul's letter to the Galatians. It's much harder, especially for Gentile Christians today, to hear how much it trades on deep assumptions, from the early church up to the Enlightenment and modern periods, that Judaism is essentially anti-freedom, that its law is necessarily a burden and a torment, that there is something fundamentally gross and wrong about circumcision, and that we Christians have escaped from a primitive phase of ancient religion with its bloody sacrifices and arbitrary laws into something much superior.

This sermon is but one example of many, and not the worst that I have heard. I have had to sit through expositions of the baptism of the Ethiopian eunuch hammering on nasty old Leviticus with no awareness of what the laws concerning eunuchs actually meant to Leviticus or, for that matter, no awareness that it was not the Apostle Philip but the prophet Isaiah who first offered another take on the status of the eunuch. And then there are all the sermons on the woman with the hemorrhage of blood—"excluded" by those terrible Old Testament purity laws, only to be restored to wholeness and community by "inclusive" Jesus.

Now that I have the ears to hear, I'm simply astounded by how easy it still is to dismiss another religion from our so-called progressive pulpits without the slightest awareness that we're doing it. It is because we Christians are so immersed in deep habits of observing, for example, the way Jesus breaks with aspects of Israel's tradition—which he surely does!—without examining with equal fervor and attention all the ways that he maintains, depends upon, thinks, and critiques from it; without recognizing, in fact, that the New Testament is incomprehensible without the Old. Or, perhaps more precisely, that the New Testament is comprehended *wrongly* without the Old, and for that reason *dangerously*.

Let me leave the reader with no doubt on the matter: I believe that Christian anti-Judaism is a noxious, toxic, and repellent aspect of Christian tradition, present in all its strains, and it has to go. If Christianity cannot be Christianity without being anti-Judaic, then it is a contradiction in terms and ought not exist at all. But if there can be a Christianity that is not anti-Judaic—and, evidently, I hope and believe there can be—then it will take an enormous work of self-examination, purification, and recalibration to preach our faith in the crucified and risen Jew Jesus without propagating the old unfortunate habits that we have inherited. I acknowledge myself, as a Christian theologian, to be only at the very beginning of this process.

Of course, how to do this, and how to do it well, is the rub. The solution is not denying genuine and deep disagreement between Christianity and Judaism: that would be merely dishonest. A start might be the recognition on the part of Christians that there was a bifurcation within the tradition of Israel that took place in the first century as a result of the twin crises of Jesus of Nazareth and the destruction of the temple in Jerusalem. This would have two implications that could serve as correctives to our anti-Judaic habits: first, the acknowledgement that rabbinic Judaism is a *legitimate* heir to the faith of Israel, a notion that most of the church through history has fiercely denied, for obvious if also usually vicious reasons; and second, that Christianity did not spring out of the empty tomb fully formed, so to speak, like Athena from the head of Zeus, but precisely in its acclamation of Jesus as Messiah and Lord, it became another, alternative continuation of Israel's faith. The apostolic church did not have the New Testament, after all—it had only the Scriptures of Israel!

And this takes me to a second proposal, which is to urge Christian reclamation of the Old Testament as truly holy Scripture. Please note that in calling it the Old Testament I am openly acknowledging that I, and we, in the church read these texts as part of our Christian Bible and cannot (and should not) pretend to take a neutral approach to the "Hebrew Scriptures."

While I advocate for strong Christian reception of Israel's Scripture, I must admit at the outset that this is not an automatic solution. While the Marcionite heresy—assigning the Old Testament to the realm of a primitive, violent God that has nothing to do with the Jesus proclaimed by the

New Testament—is openly condemned by Christian doctrine, we have no correspondingly named heresy of manipulating and flattening the Old Testament beyond recognition in order to fit Christian notions of what it ought to say, prove, or prophesy. Christians through history have certainly been quite accomplished at doing all those things.

But I wish to address my own time and the needs of my tradition at this point, and what I see far more often than flattening or manipulating the Old Testament is a refusal to deal with the Old Testament at all. Although the standard lectionary in use offers two Old Testament and two New Testament readings every Sunday (except in Easter season, where the Old Testament is replaced by Acts: the most egregious liturgical expression of supersessionism), I regularly find the two Old Testament lessons simply to be omitted, and even when included, rarely preached on. As an editor of a theological journal, I have spent more than a decade soliciting essays on Old Testament texts for each issue, and it is always a struggle: Old Testament professors can be persuaded to write, but pastors are often wary and decline.[20]

Some of the neglect, I think, is motivated by a salutary fear—the fear of "stealing" the Old Testament from the Jews or otherwise contributing to the long legacy of abuse. But I suspect at a deeper level it really is residual Marcionism, a distrust of the Old Testament and the God presented therein. The New Testament is safer and more familiar ground, and our habits of reading it apart from and even in competition with the Old Testament shield us from recognizing the misinterpretations that accrue. Thus, in my own community and tradition at this point in time, I judge ignoring the Old Testament to be more dangerous than mishandling it. At least in mishandling there is the opportunity for ears and eyes to be opened, but neglect cuts off all hope of communication. It certainly reinforces the perception of the alien otherness of Judaism in both ancient and rabbinic forms.[21]

How then to read the Old Testament well, as Christians? Do we have resources from within, a minority tradition to pose against the majority tradition, that will help us in this task? I would urge and invite a broad

20. See the insightful study by Strawn, *Old Testament Is Dying*.

21. Juel, *Messianic Exegesis*; Hays, *Echoes of Scripture in the Letters of Paul*; *Echoes of Scripture in the Gospels* are outstanding examples of reading the New Testament and Christianity in continuity with the faith of Israel rather than at its expense. I should note that Juel was my most formative teacher of the Bible; he gave back to me what the lectionary took away.

range of Christian experiments in non-supersessionist, non-anti-Judaic interpretations of our faith; I suspect we need a wide range of voices and efforts and mutual discernment on the way to reaching this goal. For my part, having already set before us a seemingly impossible task, I may as well up the ante at this point and see if use can be made of what would appear to be the least promising resource of all: the Reformer Martin Luther.[22] If he of all people can be turned to the task of mending Christian anti-Judaism, then there is perhaps hope for the Christian tradition as a whole.

It is already well documented how Luther underwent a bewildering transformation, one from his early treatise, "That Jesus Christ Was Born a Jew" (1523), to his late hateful writings, especially his infamous "On the Jews and Their Lies" (1543). In the earlier piece, Luther became the first to propose something akin to modern notions of political toleration for the Jews, offering reasons for clemency and expanded economic options. The nineteenth-century Jewish scholar Heinrich Graetz once said that Luther's early treatise offered "words of a kind that Jews had not heard for a thousand years."[23] Yet in the later work, Luther condenses a thousand years of Christian hatred and distrust of the Jews, backed by his own great fame and rhetorical fireworks. The grief of this Jekyll-and-Hyde transformation is only exacerbated by the wider historical context: for example, the fact that Luther was silent on the Jews basically from 1526 to 1538,[24] during arguably the most insightful period of his career; that he was actually on top of the scholarly literature of his day on the Jews, which was rife with what we would now call "fake news"; and that he invoked the Old Testament's punishment of idolatry by death and its extensive criticisms of Israel against the Jews of his day, equating one with the other in cases of divine wrath, but exonerating the Old Testament Jews against rabbinic Jews when the distinction suited him. In the final analysis, although in his later work Luther mostly reiterated the worst of the Christian tradition regarding the Jews, his most original contribution to Christian literature on the Jews was in fact his call to tolerate and live together with them[25]—yes, this is the same Luther who later advocated burning down their synagogues and chasing them out of town like wild dogs!

---

22. The most thorough, nuanced, and up-to-date study to address Luther's "Janus-like" attitude toward the Jews is Kaufmann, *Luther's Jews*.

23. Kaufmann, *Luther's Jews*, 135.

24. Kaufmann, *Luther's Jews*, 87.

25. Kaufmann, *Luther's Jews*, 66.

Needless to say, for a Lutheran theologian such as myself, this is an acutely painful problem that demands a response. The fact that Luther is not unique but representative impels me to urge other Christians to face up to the worst of their own distinctive and of our shared tradition.

But now it is time to try to turn this specifically Lutheran tradition against itself—to elevate the minority report to deconstruct the majority report—in making the case for the Christian tradition to embrace fully the Old Testament as holy Scripture, and for my own Lutheran community to reject its faulty hearings of both Old Testament and Luther on the law of God. Let me be clear, I am *not* claiming that the writings of Luther's that I will discuss here avoid supersessionism or disdain of rabbinic or contemporary Judaism—they don't. What I am saying is that inadvertently (very inadvertently!) they offer resources for the corrective that we need to undertake of hearing, recognizing, and honoring the Old Testament as Scripture and the law as God's word. My hope is that in so doing Christians will also find resources for the task of building a new relationship with Israel past, present, and future.

I shall focus my attention now on three writings of Luther's from the year 1525, which are not otherwise famous for addressing the relationship between Christians and Jews. Let us begin with the sarcastically entitled treatise "Against the Heavenly Prophets," a response to Luther's Wittenberg colleague Karlstadt's iconoclastic reforms.

In this work, Luther first rejects violence as a means to the reforming end—a principle we wish he had remembered later in life—and second, he asserts that the heart is not cured of its idolatry simply by removing the idol from the eye. As the third argument against Karlstadt, who urged the destruction of images because of laws to this effect in the Old Testament, Luther offers a different approach to Christian interpretation of the Old Testament.

Yes, Luther admits, graven images of God are forbidden. However, he notes that Moses was commanded to make the bronze serpent, and Joshua set up a memorial stone on the banks of the Jordan. Then Luther makes a more significant point, which he will have cause to repeat again in 1525 and later in his career: Moses gave the laws found in Exodus to the Jewish people alone. They were not given to Gentiles and have not been extended to Christians, and therefore they are not the concern of baptized Saxons.

In fact, Luther argues, those who attempt to impose Mosaic law on Gentile Christians de facto reject Christ and the gospel. Now this may seem like typical Luther hyperbole or disdain for Jewish law as such, and as I've already demonstrated, this is how such things usually play out from our pulpits even today. However, Luther here—and elsewhere, as we will shortly see—is working from two very specific verses of the New Testament, his charter for Old Testament exegesis. The first of these verses he cites at this point is Acts 15:10–11: "Now therefore why do you make trial of God by putting a yoke upon the neck of the disciples which neither our fathers nor we have been able to bear? But we believe that we shall be saved through the grace of the Lord Jesus, just as they will." Luther comments: "With this saying (as Paul with his) Peter abrogates for the Christian the whole of Moses with all his laws."[26] Note well: the problem is not the inferiority of the law of Moses or any other flaw internal to it. It is abrogated only *as a means of salvation*.

Luther then rejects the standard Christian distinction between ceremonial and judicial law on the one hand and moral law on the other. Quite the contrary, he avers that "out of the Ten Commandments flow and depend all the other commandments and the whole of Moses."[27] The ceremonies are what teach Israel to have no other gods; the civil law of Israel promotes honor to parents and punishes adultery, murder, stealing, and false witness. Neither the ceremonial nor the judicial law are dismissed by Luther as purely arbitrary or antiquated, as thinkers of the Enlightenment and onwards have tended to judge Israelite religion. Luther points out that there is ceremonial law within the Decalogue: the prohibition of images (which, by Luther's time, had been dropped from the Ten Commandments in Christian usage) and the Sabbath (which had not). Christians disregard these because of the New Testament's intervention in the tradition of Israel, as seen, for example, in Colossians 2:16–17 and Galatians 4:10–11.

This line of thought brings Luther to the other verse he will invoke most often in discussions of the law of Moses, namely Galatians 5:3: "I testify again to every man who accepts circumcision that he is obligated to keep the whole law." If Karlstadt wants to destroy graven images in the name of Moses, Luther argues, then he also must observe the Sabbath, receive circumcision, and keep every other law as well. The Torah is a seamless garment, in a sense, to be worn whole or not at all—*if* it is a means of salvation.

26. Luther, *Luther's Works* (hereafter cited as *LW*), 40:92.
27. *LW* 40:93.

But insofar as Moses's law dovetails with the natural law, neither is abrogated yet both remain in force. That which is not natural law in Moses is "free, null, and void, and is specifically given to the Jewish people alone."[28] Yet if the Decalogue is a purely local interpretation of the natural law given to the Jews and not to the Gentiles, why do Christians bother with it at all? Luther replies, "Because the natural laws were never so orderly and well written as by Moses." And indeed, Luther found far more to be useful in Moses than the Decalogue alone. "I wish," he continues, "that we would accept even more of Moses in worldly matters, such as the laws about the bill of divorce, the Sabbath year, the year of jubilee, tithes, and the like. Through such laws the world would be better governed than now with its practices in usury, trade, and marriage."[29] For that matter, although the precise day of Saturday is not required of Christians, natural law suggests the need for regular rest and refreshment, which is a sensible time also to hear and meditate on the Word of God. So long as they do not turn it into a new law upon which salvation depends, Gentiles have much to learn from the law of Moses.

In the same year (1525) Luther reworked a sermon from a preaching series on Exodus and published it as "How Christians Should Regard Moses." He begins by stating that God has delivered two public sermons: the first on Mount Sinai, delivering the law; the second on Pentecost, delivering the Holy Spirit with the preaching of the gospel. Here we find one of Luther's most straightforward elucidations of the distinction between law and gospel:

> The law commands and requires us to do certain things. The law is thus directed solely to our behavior and consists in making requirements. For God speaks through the law, saying, "Do this, avoid that, this is what I expect of you." The gospel, however, does not preach what we are to do or to avoid. It sets up no requirements but reverses the approach of the law, does the very opposite, and says, "This is what God has done for you; he has let his Son be made flesh for you, has let him be put to death for your sake." ... For the gospel teaches exclusively what has been given us by God, and not—as in the case of the law—what we are to do and give to God.[30]

28. *LW* 40:97–98.
29. *LW* 40:98.
30. *LW* 35:162.

Though Luther is in the habit of saying "the law of Moses," he goes on to emphasize that Moses received the law, as an intermediary for the Israelites, from angels ordained by God (Gal 3:19). The law is *not* a thing of merely earthly importance—much less an oppressive burden to be sloughed off by the superior Christian religion—but truly divine.

While Luther called upon the church of his day to distinguish between temporal and spiritual powers—chiefly, that bishops should not also be princes—he acknowledged that the Israelites were distinguished by having a society in which the temporal and spiritual were merged at God's command. But again, Luther emphasizes, this law was only given to the Jews, not the Gentiles. If there are aspects of their respective laws in common, it is because they both draw on the natural law.

Luther notes that he is emphasizing this point over against the "enthusiasts" who "read Moses, extol him, and bring up the way he ruled the people with commandments"[31] in order to suggest that Christians must do the exact same. Luther goes so far as to say that he would prefer never to preach again "than to let Moses return and to let Christ be torn out of our hearts."[32] This may sound once again like denigration of the Jewish law, but Luther's reasons are the same as before. First, "Moses was an intermediary solely for the Jewish people."[33] Second, alluding to Galatians 5:3 again, "If I were to accept Moses in one commandment, I would have to accept the entire Moses." He elaborates more fully with reference to the opening line of the Decalogue, observing: "God never led us out of Egypt, but only the Jews." Therefore, "We will regard Moses as a teacher, but we will not regard him as our lawgiver—unless he agrees with both the New Testament and the natural law."[34]

As in the previous treatise, Luther anticipates the question: "Why then do you preach about Moses if he does not pertain to us?"[35] Luther replies with three points to be found "in Moses" that are of value to the Christian.

The first is the usefulness of Moses's law. One can "dismiss the commandments given to the people of Israel . . . except insofar as I gladly and willingly accept something from Moses, as if I said, 'This is how Moses ruled,

31. *LW* 35:164.
32. *LW* 35:164.
33. *LW* 35:164.
34. *LW* 35:165.
35. *LW* 35:166.

and it seems fine to me, so I will follow him in this or that particular."[36] This distinction is crucial for Luther. Apart from its alignment with the natural law, there is nothing in the Mosaic law that is binding in itself on Gentiles or Christians. But there is *also* nothing about it that requires categorical rejection. A Christian need not deliberately avoid and eschew Jewish law simply because it is Jewish. Luther particularly liked the tithe over the flat tax. Still, it is not enough that God said it; what matters is whether God said it to *me*, to *us*. Something may indeed be the Word of God, but we may not in fact be the people to whom it is addressed.[37]

After discussing these good points of law found in Moses, Luther moves on to the other two valuable things found in Moses, namely "the promises and pledges of God about Christ"[38] and "the beautiful examples of faith, of love, and of the cross, as shown in the fathers, Adam, Abel, Noah, Abraham, Isaac, Jacob, Moses, and all the rest."[39] Of interest here is the fact that Luther does not attribute a "works righteousness" or "law religion" to the Israelites that was superseded by a superior Christianity—again, a common modernist assumption. Rather, the patriarchs and prophets *also* lived by faith in the promise and obeyed God as a result of that faith, not to earn salvation. Gentile Christians can profitably learn about their own faith from the Old Testament. Luther stresses in this way *continuity between Israel and church* rather than abject discontinuity. Let me flag, however, the fact that Luther would not extend the continuity between ancient Israel and rabbinic Judaism and, conflating his Roman opponents with rabbinic Jews, would take the latter to be exponents of a works-righteousness religion. We may note, then, the danger for Christians both in their self-regard and in their regard of contemporary Jews when the continuity of each with Israel is severed. *In both cases*, the corrective we need is to stress the continuity, not to sever it once and for all.

The final work from 1525 to consider is Luther's commentary on Deuteronomy. Those even slightly acquainted with Luther's theology may be surprised that the Reformer took up this of all books—and loved it. That probably says more about Lutherans' faulty reception of Luther's teaching on the law than anything else. Indeed, his task here is to rehabilitate the Old Testament from its cultured despisers. "There are many," he remarks, "and

36. *LW* 35:166.
37. *LW* 35:170.
38. *LW* 35:168.
39. *LW* 35:173.

of these some who in their own eyes are obviously masters of everything—who consider Moses and the whole Old Testament of very small value and claim to be content with the Gospel." Luther argues to the contrary that the gospel is not enough! Rather, "our Moses is the fountain and the father of all the prophets and sacred books, that is, of heavenly wisdom and eloquence." He notes how all the later prophets derived their insights from him: "From his horn of plenty all their riches have been taken."[40]

He continues with praise for the law as taught by Moses in all its forms:

> For first of all Moses teaches godliness. He preaches faith amply and richly. He attaches the most beautiful ceremonies, by which the common people must be grasped and held, to keep them from making up their own, which God hates. Then he busies himself with the ordering of civil government and the nurture of mutual love, and he directs and arranges everything with the most suitable and just laws. Nothing here is foolish or useless, but everything is necessary and useful.[41]

Here again, Luther's rejection of an artificial distinction between moral, ceremonial, and judicial law is evident. He offers a reason for the ceremonies: God realized that "the masses" tend to be most impressed by "surface displays," so, "to keep them from being empty masks and mere spectacles, He added His Word, the stuff and substance behind the masks, as it were, that by it they might become serious and meaningful." Note well: this means that the ceremonies of Moses were *not* mere masks and spectacles but rather true vehicles of God's Word.

Luther keeps up his praise of the law of Moses throughout the commentary. Deuteronomy is "a most ample and excellent explanation of the Decalogue. After you know it, you would want nothing more that is needful for understanding the Ten Commandments."[42] The Shema is a declaration of the gospel that elicits obedience to the law: "When [Moses] says: 'You shall love the Lord,' he arouses joyous and free service to God. For when I love God truly, I want everything God wants; nor is anything sweeter than to hear and to do what God wants." He further observes, "If I loved God with my whole heart, nothing would offend me more than contempt for the

---

40. *LW* 9:6.

41. *LW* 9:6–7.

42. *LW* 9:14.

Commandments of God."[43] In reference to Deuteronomy 10:16 ("Circumcise, therefore, the foreskin of your heart"), Luther comments,

> Amazing indeed is the legislator who at one and the same time commands works and yet condemns them when they are done! But He does this that they may know that the Law is fulfilled, not by works of the Law but from the circumcision of the heart, and that such good works are truly good only when they proceed, not from the compulsion of the Law but from the heart which was circumcised before.[44]

Here again Luther sees already in Moses a polemic against both "works righteousness" *and* antinomianism. Obedience to the law starts from the inside, with love for God. Israel's faith worked this way every bit as much as the church's: it was not inferior, primitive, or false.

Even if the gospel is what motivates true obedience, the preaching of the law remains a necessary office and an honorable one. Luther argues that Deuteronomy 18:15 forecasts Jesus, but it also establishes "those two ministries of the Word which are necessary for the salvation of the human race: the ministry of the Law and the ministry of the Gospel, one for death and the other for life. They are indeed alike if you are looking at their authority, but most unlike if you are thinking about their fruit." The difference is that Moses "demands, but he does not give what he demands."[45] (Here, as elsewhere, "Moses" is a synecdoche for the law.) The gospel through Christ by contrast gives and forgives, freely and apart from human merit; yet it too tends toward obedience to God, precisely in giving what God demands. As Luther would observe a few years later in the Large Catechism: "The Creed . . . is given in order to help us do what the Ten Commandments require of us."[46]

This commentary is not free of anti-Jewish remarks, although here we see again that the issue for Luther is not Judaism/Old Testament/Israel in itself, but what it can be or mean after Jesus. Commenting on Deuteronomy 21:15–17, about the two wives, one loved and the other unloved, he writes:

> The two wives of one man are that double and yet single church consisting of Jews and Gentiles. The hated one is the synagogue, because it killed the prophets and crucified Christ, etc.; the beloved

43. *LW* 9:68.

44. *LW* 9:110–11.

45. *LW* 9:178.

46. Luther, "Large Catechism," 431.

> one is the Gentile church, because it received the Word with joy.
> Nevertheless, the synagog has the birthright, because from it, and
> not from the Gentiles, came Christ, the apostles, and the Word.
> For salvation is of the Jews (John 4:22); therefore the Jews are not
> to be despised nowadays either, because from them, not from us,
> comes all glory, as Paul says in Rom. 9:3ff. For they were the first
> Christians, and to them were promised and entrusted the oracles
> of God (Rom 3:2).[47]

It is backhanded compliment, to be sure. At a minimum Luther argues here against despising the Jews of his own day, in honor of their past, even if there is no present election remaining to them. He will not stay the course with this argument, but it is remarkable that he ever made it at all. This is definitely a case where the minority report should be elevated against the majority report.

Despite these alarming heralds of what was to come, the commentary concludes with renewed praise for Moses and his greatness for speaking with God face to face. Luther wraps up with the assertion that "nothing greater can be taught and transmitted, so far as laws are concerned, than the Law of Moses. For all things reach their climax in him, except that the great Law was to give way to the even greater Gospel."[48] It is the nature of the Christian faith itself to elevate the gospel of Jesus Christ in this way. But Luther gives us an indication of how we *as Christians* can attempt to do so without a corresponding denigration or rejection of either the Old Testament or the law, the Torah, of the Lord God of Israel.

Thus what we need to take from Luther's minority report—and any other minority reports we can gather from the Christian tradition offering a more excellent way of regarding the Jews, starting of course with Paul's high esteem of the Jews in Romans 9–11—is the material for what the Jewish theologian Peter Ochs calls "another reformation."[49] This is a reconfiguring, reordering, and indeed reforming of the Christian practice of scriptural reading by means of a commitment to non-supersessionism: namely, refusing any longer to read the Scripture, including the New Testament, as though Israel were no longer God's covenant partner, and is now fully and totally replaced by the (Gentile) church. Ochs describes at length the efforts of postliberal Christian theologians in particular to engage in

47. *LW* 9:214–15.

48. *LW* 9:311.

49. Ochs, *Another Reformation*.

the work of "repair"[50] of the seminal breach between Israel and church two millennia ago. It is an encouraging sign that Ochs recognizes the efforts of Lutherans especially in charting a course for reversing the damage of long-standing Christian anti-Judaism.[51]

Permit me to conclude this section by demonstrating how it connects back to the first two sections on the transmission of a tradition to different cultures and the struggle with new questions being posed to the tradition. In Acts 15 we hear of a controversy among the early believers in Jesus in Jerusalem:

> Some men came down from Judea and were teaching the brothers, "Unless you are circumcised according to the custom of Moses, you cannot be saved." And after Paul and Barnabas had no small dissension and debate with them, Paul and Barnabas and some of the others were appointed to go up to Jerusalem to the apostles and the elders about this question. . . . Some believers who belonged to the party of the Pharisees rose up and said, "It is necessary to circumcise them and to order them to keep the law of Moses." (Acts 15:1–2, 5)

As the sermon I quoted from earlier shows, it is sadly quite easy for (mostly Gentile) Christians to dismiss the Pharisees' claim. But having the retrospective view of church history that the Pharisees lacked, I think we need to grant them a legitimate concern. If Israel had always known and identified the Lord by the law that they kept, how could they be confident that it would really be the *same* Lord who had called Israel into fellowship with himself that was being worshipped by the Gentiles—especially if they did not keep that same law? Would it still *really* be faith in the same God of Israel, understood to be also the Father of our Lord Jesus Christ, that the nations were worshipping as Israel's faith crossed national and cultural boundaries? Peter and James and Paul and the other apostles had

---

50. See especially Ochs, *Another Reformation*, 14–17.

51. Ochs devotes full chapters to American Lutherans George Lindbeck and Robert W. Jenson, and refers to them again, along with German Lutheran Gerhard Sauter, in the final chapter. Ochs mentions that "Lutheran theologians are disproportionately represented among the strongest Christian critics of supersessionism and the strongest advocates of deep theological engagement with Judaism" (Ochs, *Another Reformation*, 71). Some other helpful studies of interest trying to extract a way forward for Lutheran Christian theology's reclamation of the Old Testament from the mixed bag of Luther's writings include Helmer, "Luther's Trinitarian Hermeneutic"; Lindbeck, "Martin Luther and the Rabbinic Mind"; Hinlicky, "Lutheran Contribution"; Mattox, "From Faith to the Text and Back Again"; MacDonald, "Trinitarian Palimpsest."

no choice but to confront this very new question—on top of the already controversial question of whether the crucified Jesus was the promised Messiah at all. Subsequent generations' forgetfulness about Israel—which is nowhere mentioned in our standard creeds, for example—have proven the Pharisees' anxiety well-founded. All of these challenges to tradition are intimately connected to one another.

CONCLUSION: COUNT YOUR DEMONS

At some level, all three of the cases that I have examined in this chapter have to do with questioning the way things have been done in a tradition and doing them in a different way or replacing them with something else. Let me conclude with a brief reflection on one of the strangest and least popular of Jesus' parables, but one pertinent to our discussion:

> When the unclean spirit has gone out of a person, it passes through waterless places seeking rest, but finds none. Then it says, "I will return to my house from which I came." And when it comes, it finds the house empty, swept, and put in order. Then it goes and brings with it seven other spirits more evil than itself, and they enter and dwell there, and the last state of that person is worse than the first. So also will it be with this evil generation. (Matt 12:43–45)

An honest reckoning forces us who live in and from our faith traditions to recognize that sometimes they come to be inhabited by demons. It is imperative upon us to cast those demons out. But in so doing, we can't leave the house empty and suppose we have done the job. All we do then is create a vacuum, a sweet spot not only for the first demon but also possibly for its seven worse companions to come and take up a much more vicious residence.

In perceiving and decrying our demons, those outside our traditions fairly demand of us that we exorcise them. But those on the outside often *also* demand that our houses sit empty, supposing that we will live more comfortably in the emptiness, free of all tradition, all claims, all demands of the past. I am persuaded that this is a lie. The alternative is never no tradition, only a different tradition. And it's possible, not to say likely, that what replaces our one demon will be seven times worse.

But that is no excuse to tolerate the one demon. It's our business and no one else's to recognize our failings, confess them, and rectify them. But we cannot engage our traditions only destructively; we must engage them constructively as well, prudently and patiently making them more deserving of a vital future. In doing so, we will build up a house that is a true shelter for people to live in and from, a blessing to the world, and a fitting witness to the God whose mercy is everlasting.

Bibliography

Adūnīs. *Al-Thābit wa-al-mutahawwil: bahth fī al-ibdāʿ wa-al-ittibāʿ ʿinda al-ʿArab.* Beirut: Dār al-Sāqī, 2006.

Al-Azmeh, Aziz. *Arabic Thought and Islamic Societies.* London: Croom Helm, 1986.

———. *Islams and Modernities.* London: Verso, 2009.

Al-Ghazālī, Abū Hāmid b. Muhammad. *Ihyāʾ ʿulūm al-dīn.* 5 vols. Beirut: Dār al-Kutub al-ʿIlmīya, 2001.

———. *Kitāb sharh ʿajāʾib al-qalb: The Marvels of the Heart. Book 21 of the Revival of the Religious Sciences.* Translated by Walter James Skellie. Louisville: Fons Vitae, 2010.

Al-Jābirī, Muhammad ʿĀbid, and William Dowell. *Arab-Islamic Philosophy: A Contemporary Critique.* Translated by Aziz Abbassi. Austin, TX: Center for Middle Eastern Studies 1999.

Al-Khalīl ibn Ahmad al-Farāhīdī. *Kitāb al-ʿAyn.* Edited by ʿAbd al-Hamīd Hindāwī. Beirut: Dār al-Kutub al-ʿIlmīya, 2003.

Altmann, Alexander. *Moses Mendelssohn: A Biographical Study.* London: Routledge & Kegan Paul, 1973.

Asad, Talal. "Thinking about Tradition, Religion, and Politics in Egypt Today." *Critical Inquiry* 42.1 (2015) 166–214.

Augustine. *Confessions.* Translated by R. S. Pine-Coffin. New York: Penguin, 1961.

Aynde, Cemil. *The Idea of the Muslim World: A Global Intellectual History.* Cambridge: Harvard University Press, 2017.

Baubérot, Jean. "Secularization, Secularism, and Laïcité." *Empan* 2 (2013) 31–38.

Bauman, Zygmunt. *Liquid Modernity.* Cambridge: Polity, 2000.

Bell, Daniel. *The Cultural Contradictions of Capitalism.* 2nd ed. London: Heinemann, 1979.

Berger, Peter. *The Capitalist Revolution: Fifty Propositions about Prosperity, Equality, and Liberty.* New York: Basic, 1986.

———. *The Heretical Imperative: Contemporary Possibilities of Religious Affirmation.* Garden City, NY: Anchor, 1979.

———. *The Many Altars of Modernity: Toward a New Paradigm for Religion in a Pluralist Age.* Boston: de Gruyter, 2014.

Berlinerblau, Jacques. *Secularism on the Edge: Rethinking Church-State Relations in the United States, France, and Israel.* New York: Palgrave Macmillan, 2014.

Bettini, Maurizio. *Radici: tradizioni, identità, memoria.* Bologna: Il Mulino, 2016.

Blond, Philip. *Post-Secular Philosophy.* New York: Routledge, 1998.

Bourdieu, Pierre. *The Field of Cultural Production: Essays on Art and Literature*. Edited by Randall Johnson. New York: Columbia University Press, 1993.

Branch, Lori. "Post-Secular Studies." In *Routledge Companion to Literature and Religion*, edited by Mark Knight, 91–101. New York: Routledge, 2016.

Braybrooke, Marcus. *Pilgrimage of Hope: One Hundred Years of Global Interfaith Dialogue*. London: SCM, 1992.

Brodeur, Patrice. "From the Margins to the Center: The Increasing Relevance of the Global Interfaith Movement." *CrossCurrents* 55 (2005) 42–53.

Bruce, Steve. *Secularization: In Defense of an Unfashionable Theory*. Oxford: Oxford University Press, 2015.

Bryan, Christopher. "Holy Traditions and Scholarly Inquiries." *Sewanee Theological Review* 37 (1993) 2–8.

Buber, Martin. "Dialogue." In *Between Man and Man*, translated by Ronald Gregor Smith, 1–39. New York: MacMillan, 1947.

Celestine I. "Epistola 4. Ad Episcopos Provinciae Viennensis et Narbonensis." In vol. 50 of *Patrologia Latina*, edited by J.-P. Migne, 429–36. 217 vols. Paris, 1844–1864.

Chadwick, Henry. *Early Christian Thought and the Classical Tradition*. Oxford: Clarendon, 1966.

Chambers, R. W. *Thomas More*. Ann Arbor, MI: University of Michigan Press, 1973.

Clancy, Finbarr. "Breathing with Both Her Lungs: Yves Congar and Dialogue with the East." *Louvain Studies* 29 (2004) 320–49.

Cohn-Sherbok, Dan, ed. *Islam in a World of Diverse Faiths*. Basingstoke: Macmillan, 1991.

Congar, Yves. "*Magisterium*, Theologians, and the Faithful." *Doctrine and Life* 31 (1981) 548–64.

———. *The Meaning of Tradition*. 1964. Reprint, San Francisco: Ignatius, 2004.

———. "Towards a Catholic Synthesis." *Concilium* 148 (1981) 68–80.

———. *Tradition and Traditions: An Historical and a Theological Essay*. New York: Macmillan, 1967.

———. *True and False Reform in the Church*. Translated by Paul Philibert. Collegeville, MN: Michael Glazier, 2010.

Connelly, John. *From Enemy to Brother: The Revolution in Catholic Teaching on the Jews*. Cambridge, MA: Harvard University Press, 2012.

Cornille, Catherine, ed. *The Wiley-Blackwell Companion to Inter-Religious Dialogue*. Malden, MA: Wiley & Sons, 2013.

Daigle-Williamson, Marsha. "Tradition and Lewis's Individual Talent." *Christian Scholars' Review* 27 (1998) 490–505.

Denzinger, Heinrich, ed. *Enchiridion symbolorum definitinum et declarationum de rebus fidei morum / Compendium of Creeds, Definitions, and Declarations on Matters of Faith and Morals*. 43rd ed. San Francisco: Ignatius, 2010.

Dillon, Michele. *Postsecular Catholicism: Relevance and Renewal*. Oxford: Oxford University Press, 2018.

Dulles, Avery. "The Freedom of Theology." *First Things* (May 2008) 19–23.

———. "Successio Apostolorum: Successio prophetarum—Successio doctorum." *Concilium* 8 (1981) 61–67.

Dupuis, Jacques. "The Cosmic Christ in the Early Fathers." *Indian Journal of Theology* 15 (1966) 106–20.

Eck, Diane. *A New Religious America: How a "Christian Country" Has Now Become the World's Most Religiously Diverse Nation*. San Francisco: Harper Collins, 2002.

Eisenstadt, S. N. *Multiple Modernities*. 2002. Reprint, New York: Routledge, 2017.

———. "Post-Traditional Societies and the Continuity and Reconstruction of Tradition." *Daedalus* 102 (1973) 1–27.

Eisenstadt, S. N., and Stephen Richards Graubard, eds. *Intellectuals and Tradition*. New York: Humanities, 1973.

Eliot, T. S. "Murder in the Cathedral." In *The Complete Poems and Plays*, 173–221. New York: Harcourt, Brace & World, 1971.

Elon, Amos. *The Pity of it All: A Portrait of the Jews in Germany, 1743–1933*. London: Penguin, 2004.

Epp, Eldon Jay. *Junia: The First Woman Apostle*. Minneapolis: Fortress, 2005.

Faggioli, Massimo. *A Council for a Global Church: Receiving Vatican II*. Minneapolis: Fortress, 2008.

Firestone, Reuven, et al., eds. *Learned Ignorance: Intellectual Humility Among Jews, Christians, and Muslims*. Oxford: Oxford University Press, 2011.

Flannery, Austin, ed. *Vatican II: The Conciliar and Post-Conciliar Documents*. Vol. 1. New rev. ed. Northport, NY: Costello, 2004.

Fleck, Ludwik. *Genesis and Development of a Scientific Fact*. Edited by Thaddeus J. Trenn and Robert King Merton. Translated by Fred Bradley and Thaddeus J. Trenn. Chicago: University of Chicago Press, 1979.

France, Alan. *Understanding Youth in Late Modernity*. Maidenhead: Open University, 2007.

Friedman, Thomas. *Thank You For Being Late: An Optimist's Guide to Thriving in the Age of Accelerations*. New York: Farrar, Straus & Giroux, 2016.

Fromherz, Allen James. *Qatar: A Modern History*. Washington, DC: Georgetown University Press, 2017.

Gaillardetz, Richard. *By What Authority: A Primer on Scripture, the Magisterium, and the Sense of the Faithful*. Collegeville, MN: Liturgical, 2003.

———. *By What Authority? Foundations for Understanding Authority in the Church*. Collegeville, MN: Liturgical, 2018.

———, ed. *When the Magisterium Intervenes: The Magisterium and Theologians in Today's Church*. Collegeville, MN: Liturgical, 2012.

Gary, Heather Grennan. "What Women Theologians Have Done for the Church." *US Catholic* 78 (2013) 12–17.

Gassmann, Gynther. "Scripture, Tradition, and the Church: The Ecumenical Nexus in Faith and Order Work." *Journal of Ecumenical Studies* 28 (1991) 435–47.

Gilbert, Christopher. "The Archived Wisdom of a Twenty-Something Missionary." *Missio Apostolica* 16.2 (2008) 148–56.

———. *Beyond Empires*. DVD. Directed by Christopher Gilbert. New South Wales, Australia: Lamp Post, 2014.

Gilley, Sheridan. *Newman and His Age*. London: Christian Classics, 1990.

Goodman, Lenn E. *Religious Pluralism and Values in the Public Square*. New York: Cambridge University Press, 2014.

Gorski, Philip S., and Ates Altinordu. "After Secularization?" *Annual Review of Sociology* 34 (2008) 55–85.

Grabus, Nedzad. "Islamic Theology between Tradition and Challenge of Modernity." *Islam and Christian-Muslim Relations* 23 (2012) 267–77.

Graham, William A. "Traditionalism in Islam: An Essay in Interpretation." *Journal of Interdisciplinary History* 23 (1993) 496–97.

Gramsci, Antonio. *Selections from the Prison Notebooks of Antonio Gramsci*. Edited by Quintin Hoare and Geoffrey Nowell-Smith. New York: International, 2014.

Gregory, Brad. *The Unintended Reformation: How a Religious Revolution Secularized Society*. Cambridge, MA: Belknap Press of Harvard University Press, 2010.

Grob, Leonard, and John K. Roth, eds. *Encountering the Stranger: A Jewish-Christian-Muslim Trialogue*. Seattle: University of Washington Press, 2012.

Grosby, Stephen. "Tradition in the Work of Shils and Polanyi: A Few Comments." *Tradition and Discovery* 39 (2013) 38–42.

Habermas, Jürgen. "Secularism's Crisis of Faith: Notes on Post-Secular Society." *New Perspectives Quarterly* 25 (2008) 17–29.

Haj, Samira. *Reconfiguring Islamic Tradition: Reform, Rationality, and Modernity*. Stanford, CA: Stanford University Press, 2009.

Ḥanafī, Ḥasan. *Al-Turāth wa-al-tajdīd: mawqifunā min al-turāth al-qadīm*. Cairo: Maktabat al-Anglū-al-Miṣrīya, 1987.

Hartlin, Patrick J. "*Sensus Fidelium*: A Roman Catholic Reflection on its Significance for Ecumenical Thought." *Journal of Ecumenical Studies* 28 (1991) 74–87.

Harvey, David. *The Condition of Postmodernity: An Enquiry into the Origins of Cultural Change*. Cambridge, MA: Blackwell, 1989.

Hays, Richard B. *Echoes of Scripture in the Gospels*. Waco, TX: Baylor University Press, 2017.

———. *Echoes of Scripture in the Letters of Paul*. New Haven, CT: Yale University Press, 1993.

Heaphy, Brian. *Late Modernity and Social Change: Reconstructing Social and Personal Life*. New York: Routledge, 2007.

Heft, James. *John XXII (1316–1334) and Papal Teaching Authority*. New York: Edwin Mellen, 1986.

———. "'Sensus fidelium' and the Marian Dogmas." In *Mater Fidei et Fidelium: Collected Essays to Honor Theodore Koehler on His 80th Birthday*, edited by Johann Roten, 767–85. Marian Library Studies 17–23. Dayton, OH: University of Dayton, 1991.

Helmer, Christine. "Luther's Trinitarian Hermeneutic and the Old Testament." *Modern Theology* 18.1 (2002) 49–73.

Herbel, Oliver. *Turning to Tradition: Converts and the Making of an American Orthodox Church*. New York: Oxford University Press, 2014.

Hertzberg, Arthur. *The French Enlightenment and the Jews*. New York: Columbia University Press, 1968.

Hervieu-Leger, Daniele. "Tradition, Innovation, and Modernity: Research Notes." *Social Compass* 36 (1989) 71–81.

Hinlicky, Paul R. "A Lutheran Contribution to the Theology of Judaism." *Journal of Ecumenical Studies* 31.1–2 (1994) 123–52.

Hobsbawn, Eric, and Terence Ranger, eds. *The Invention of Tradition*. 1st ed. Cambridge: Cambridge University Press, 1984.

Hourani, George Fadlo. *Reason and Tradition in Islamic Ethics*. Cambridge: Cambridge University Press, 1985.

Howard, Thomas Albert. *The Faiths of Others: Modern History and the Rise of Interreligious Dialogue*. New Haven, CT: Yale University Press, forthcoming.

———. *The Pope and the Professor: Pius IX, Ignaz von Döllinger, and the Quandary of the Modern Age*. Oxford: Oxford University Press, 2017.

BIBLIOGRAPHY

———. *Religion and the Rise of Historicism*. Cambridge: Cambridge University Press, 1999.

Hudson, D. Dennis. *Protestant Origins in India: Tamil Evangelical Christians, 1706–1835*. Grand Rapids: Eerdmans, 2000.

Hume, G. B. "Development of Marriage Teaching." *Origins* 10 (1980) 275–77.

Hunter, James Davison. *To Change the World: The Irony, Tragedy, and Possibility of Christianity in the Late Modern World*. New York: Oxford University Press, 2010.

Ibn Ḥajar al-ʿAsqalānī, Aḥmad ibn ʿAlī, et al. *Fatḥ al-bārī: sharḥ Ṣaḥīḥ al-Bukhārī*. 15 vols. Sidon/Beirut: al-Maktaba al-ʿAṣrīya, 2007.

Ibn Khaldūn, ʿAbd al-Raḥmān ibn Muhammad. *Muqaddimah Ibn Khaldūn*. Edited by Darwīsh al-Juwaydī. Ṣayda/Beirut: al-Maktaba al-ʿAṣrīya, 2000.

Iggers, Georg. "Historicism: The History and Meaning of the Term." *Journal of the History of Ideas* 56 (1995) 129–55.

International Theological Commission (ITC). "Theology Today: Perspectives, Principles, and Criteria." *Origins* 41.40 (2012) 641–60.

Jackson, Sherman A. *Islam and the Problem of Black Suffering*. New York: Oxford University Press, 2009.

Jadʿān, Fahmī. *Naẓarīyat al-turāth wa-dirāsāt ʿArabīya wa-Islāmīya ukhrá*. Amman: Wizārat al-Thaqāfa, 2010.

Jeyaraj, Daniel. *Bartholomäus Ziegenbalg: The Father of Modern Protestant Mission: An Indian Assessment*. New Delhi and Chennai: Indian Society for Promoting Christian Knowledge and Gurukul Lutheran Theological College and Research Institute, 2006.

John Paul II. *Crossing the Threshold of Faith*. Edited by Vittorio Messori. New York: Alfred Knopf, 1995.

———. "On Catholic Universities." August 15, 1990. Online. http://w2.vatican.va/content/john-paul-ii/en/apost_constitutions/documents/hf_jp-ii_apc_15081990_ex-corde-ecclesiae.html.

Johnson, Elizabeth. *Quest for the Living God: Mapping Frontiers in the Theology of God*. New York: Continuum, 2008.

Juel, Donald. *Messianic Exegesis: Christological Interpretation of the Old Testament in Early Christianity*. Minneapolis: Augsburg Fortress, 1998.

Juynboll, G. H. A., and D. W. Brown. "Sunna." In *Encyclopaedia of Islam*, edited by H. A. R. Gibb and P. J. Bearman, 878–81. New ed. Leiden: Brill, 1997.

Kaufmann, Thomas. *Luther's Jews: A Journey into Anti-Semitism*. Translated by Lesley Sharpe and Jeremy Noakes. Oxford: Oxford University Press, 2017.

Kayaoglu, Turan. "Explaining Interfaith Dialogue in the Muslim World." *Religion and Politics* 8 (2015) 1–27.

Kendall, Elisabeth, and Ahmad Kahn, eds. *Reclaiming Islamic Tradition: Modern Interpretations of the Classical Heritage*. Edinburgh: Edinburgh University Press, 2016.

Ker, Ian. *John Henry Newman: A Biography*. Oxford: Oxford University Press, 1988.

———. "Wisdom of the Future." *Tablet*, September 18, 2010. 14–15.

Kerr, Fergus. "A Different World: Neo-Scholasticism and its Discontents." *International Journal of Systematic Theology* 8 (2006) 128–48.

Kirk, Kathleen. *The "Sensus Fidelium," with Special Reference to the Thought of Blessed John Henry Newman*. Leominster: Gracewing, 2010.

Kolb, Robert. "The Three-Hundredth Anniversary of Lutheran Mission in India." *Lutheran Quarterly* 21.1 (2007) 95–101.

Komonchak, Joseph. "The Catholic University in the Church." In *Catholic Universities in Church and Society: A Dialogue on Ex corde ecclesiae,* edited by John P. Langan, 35–73. Washington, DC: Georgetown University Press, 1993.

———. "Modernity and the Construction of Roman Catholicism." *Cristianismo nella Storia* 18 (1997) 353–85.

Kretzmann, O. P. "Blueprint for Christ College." 1964. Online. https://www.valpo.edu/christ-college/files/2017/05/BLUEPRINT-OF-CHRIST-COLLEGE.pdf.

———. "The Destiny of a Christian University in the Modern World." In *The Lutheran Reader,* edited by Paul J. Contino and David Morgan, 109–116. Valparaiso, IN: Valparaiso University, 1999.

Lamb, Matthew L., and Matthew Levering, eds. *The Reception of Vatican II.* New York: Oxford University Press, 2017.

———. *Vatican II: Renewal within Tradition.* Oxford: Oxford University Press, 2008.

Larson, Per. *Bishop Josiah Kibira of Bukoba in an International Perspective.* Nairobi and Dodoma: Uzima and Central Tanganyika, n.d.

Lash, Nicholas. *Seeing in the Dark: University Sermons.* London: Darton Longman & Todd, 2005.

Ledwith, Miceal. "The Theology of Tradition in the World Council of Churches." *Irish Theological Quarterly* 43.2 (1976) 104–123.

Legaspi, Michael C. *The Death of Scripture and the Rise of Biblical Studies.* Oxford: Oxford University Press, 2010.

Lindbeck, George. "Martin Luther and the Rabbinic Mind." In *Understanding the Rabbinic Mind: Essays on the Hermeneutic of Max Kadushim,* edited by Peter Ochs, 141–64. Atlanta: Scholars Press for South Florida Studies in the History of Judaism, 1990.

———. *The Nature of Doctrine: Religion and Theology in a Postliberal Age.* Philadelphia: Westminster, 1984.

Lucy, Seán. *T. S. Eliot and the Idea of Tradition.* New York: Barnes & Noble, 1960.

Luther, Martin. "The Large Catechism." In *The Book of Concord: The Confessions of the Evangelical Lutheran Church,* edited by Robert Kolb and Timothy J. Wengert, 377–480. Minneapolis: Fortress, 2000.

———. *Luther's Works.* 82 vols. Edited by J. Pelikan and H. Lehmann. American ed. St. Louis: Concordia; Philadelphia: Fortress, 1955.

Lutz, Jessie Gregory, and Salah El-Shakhs. *Tradition and Modernity: The Role of Traditionalism in the Modernization Process.* Washington, DC: University Press of America, 1982.

Lyotard, Jean-Francois. *The Postmodern Condition: A Report on the State of Knowledge.* Translated by Brian Massumi. Minneapolis: University of Minnesota Press, 1984.

MacDonald, Nathan. "A Trinitarian Palimpsest: Luther's Reading of the Priestly Blessing (Numbers 6:24–26)." *Pro Ecclesia* 21.3 (2012) 299–313.

MacIntyre, Alasdair. *Three Rival Forms of Moral Enquiry: Encyclopedia, Genealogy, and Tradition.* Notre Dame, IN: University of Notre Dame Press, 1990.

———. *Whose Justice?, Which Rationality?* Notre Dame, IN: University of Notre Dame Press, 1988.

Mahdavi, Mojtaba. "Muslims and Modernities: From Islamism to Post-Islamism?" *Religious Studies and Theology* 32 (2013) 57–71.

Mahmood, Saba. *Politics of Piety: The Islamic Revival and the Feminist Subject*. Princeton, NJ: Princeton University Press, 2012.

———. "Secularism, Hermeneutics, and Empire: The Politics of Islamic Reformation." *Public Culture* 18 (2006) 323–47.

Majlisī, Muḥammad Bāqir ibn Muḥammad Taqī. *Biḥār al-anwār: al-jāmiʿah li-durar akhbār al-aʾimmah al-aṭhār, al-Ṭabʿah*. 2nd ed. Beirut: Dār al-ʿĀmira, 2011.

Marcel, Gabriel. *Creative Fidelity*. New York: Farrar, Straus & Giroux, 1964.

Marx, Karl, and Friedrich Engels. *Communist Manifesto*. Translated by Gareth Stedman Jones. New York: Penguin, 1967.

Matheson, Peter. *Argula von Grumbach: A Woman's Voice in the Reformation*. Edinburgh: T&T Clark, 1995.

———. *Argula von Grumbach (1492–1554/7): A Woman before Her Time*. Eugene, OR: Cascade, 2013.

Mattox, Mickey L. "From Faith to the Text and Back Again: Martin Luther on the Trinity in the Old Testament." *Pro Ecclesia* 15.3 (2006) 281–303.

Meilaender, Gilbert. "Conscience and Authority." *First Things* (November 2007) 30–34.

Mendelssohn, Moses. *Jerusalem: On Religious Power and Judaism*. Translated by A. Arkush. Hanover, NH: University Press of New England, 1983.

Micklethwait, John, and Adrian Woolridge. *God Is Back: How the Global Revival of Faith Is Changing the World*. New York: Penguin, 2010.

Mirsepassi, Ali, and Tadd Graham Fernée. *Islam, Democracy, and Cosmopolitanism: At Home and in the World*. New York: Cambridge University Press, 2014.

Moosa, Ebrahim, and Sherali Tareen. "Revival and Reform." In *The Princeton Encyclopedia of Islamic Political Thought*, edited by Gerhard Bowering, 462–70. Princeton, NJ: Princeton University Press, 2013.

Morrow, Jeffrey L. "'The Acid of History: La Peyrere, Hobbes, Spinoza, and the Separation of Faith and Reason in Modern Biblical Studies." *Heythrop Journal* 58 (2017) 169–80.

Mueller, Joseph G. "Forgetting as a Principle of Continuity in Tradition." *Theological Studies* 70 (2009) 751–81.

Ndoumai, Pierre. "Justin Martyr et le dialogue interreligieux contemporain." *Laval théologique et philosophique* 66 (2010) 547–64.

Netton, Ian Richard. *Islam, Christianity, and Tradition: A Comparative Exploration*. Edinburgh: Edinburgh University Press, 2006.

Neville, Robert C. *Religion in Late Modernity*. Albany, NY: State University of New York Press, 2002.

Newman, John Henry. *Apologia pro Vita Sua*. Edited by Martin J. Svaglic. Oxford: Clarendon, 1967.

———. *An Essay on the Development of Christian Doctrine*. Leominster, Herefordshire: Gracewing, 2018.

———. *Conscience, Consensus, and the Development of Doctrine*. Edited by James Gaffney. New York: Image, 1992.

———. *On Consulting the Faithful in Matters of Doctrine*. Edited by John Coulson. London: Sheed and Ward, 1961.

———. *The Letters and Diaries of John Henry Newman*. Oxford: Clarendon, 1973.

Nichols, Aidan. "T. S. Eliot and Yves Congar on the Nature of Tradition." *Angelicum* 61 (1984) 473–85.

Novak, David. *The Election of Israel*. Cambridge: Cambridge University Press, 1995.

———. *The Jewish Social Contract.* Princeton, NJ: Princeton University Press, 2005.

———. *The Theology of Nahmanides Systematically Presented.* Atlanta: Scholars, 1992.

Ochs, Peter. *Another Reformation: Postliberal Christianity and the Jews.* Grand Rapids: Baker Academic, 2011.

O'Collins, Gerald. "Art of the Possible." *Tablet,* July 14, 2012. 6–7.

———. *The Second Vatican Council on Other Religions.* Oxford: Oxford University Press, 2013.

Oesterreicher, John. *The New Encounter between Christians and Jews.* New York: Philosophical Library, 1985.

O'Malley, John W. "A Lesson for Today? Bishops and Theologians at the Council of Trent." *America* 205 (2011) 11–31.

———. *Trent: What Happened at the Council?* Cambridge, MA: Harvard University Press, 2013.

———. *What Happened at Vatican II?* Cambridge, MA: Harvard University Press, 2010.

Osterhammel, Jürgen. *The Transformation of the World: A Global History of the Nineteenth Century.* Translated by Patrick Camiller. Princeton, NJ: Princeton University Press, 2009.

Otten, Willemien. "Authority and Identity in the Transition from Monastic to Scholastic Theology: Peter Abelard and Bernard of Clairvaux." In *Religious Identity and the Problem of Historical Foundation: The Foundational Character of Authoritative Sources in the History of Christianity and Judaism,* edited by Judith Fisherman, 349–68. Leiden: Brill, 2004.

Pelikan, Jaroslav. *The Christian Tradition: A History of the Development of Doctrine.* Chicago: University of Chicago Press, 1971.

———. *The Vindication of Tradition.* New Haven, CT: Yale University Press, 1984.

Pieper, Josef. *Tradition: Concept and Claim.* Translated by E. Christian Kopff. South Bend, IN: St. Augustine's, 2010.

Polanyi, Michael. *Personal Knowledge.* Chicago: University of Chicago Press, 1958.

———. *The Tacit Dimension.* New York: Doubleday, 1966.

Pratt, Douglas. *The Church and Other Faiths: The World Council of Churches, the Vatican, and Interreligious Dialogue.* Bern: Peter Lang, 2010.

Queiruga, Andres Torres. "*Magisterium* and Theology: Principles and Facts." In *Concilium: Theology and Magisterium,* edited by Felix Wilfred and Susan A. Ross, 51–63. London: SCM, 2012.

Rahman, Fazlur. *Islam & Modernity: Transformation of an Intellectual Tradition.* Chicago: University of Chicago Press, 1984.

Rawls, John. *Political Liberalism.* New York: Columbia University Press, 1993.

———. *A Theory of Justice.* Rev. ed. Cambridge, MA: Harvard University Press, 1999.

Roggema, Barbara, et al. *The Three Rings: Textual Studies in the Historical Trialogue of Judaism, Christianity, and Islam.* Leuven: Peeters, 2005.

Rolheiser, Ronald. *Wrestling with God.* New York: Penguin Random House, 2018.

Rombs, Ronnie J., and Alexander Y. Hwang, eds. *Tradition & the Rule of Faith in the Early Church: Essays in Honor of Joseph T. Lienhard, SJ.* Washington: Catholic University of America Press, 2011.

Rosenberg, Harold. *Discovering the Present.* Chicago: University of Chicago Press, 1973.

Sacks, Elias. *Moses Mendelssohn's Living Script.* Bloomington, IN: Indiana University Press, 2017.

Sacks, Jonathan. *Not in God's Name: Confronting Religious Violence.* New York: Schocken, 2015.

———. *One People?: Tradition, Modernity, and Jewish Unity.* London: Littman, 1993.

"Sacra Congregatio Pro Doctrina Fidei." *Acta Apostolicae Sedis* 65 (1973) 396–408.

Sajed, Alina. "Late Modernity/Postmodernity." In vol. 8 of *International Studies Encyclopedia*, edited by Robert Denemarkm, et al., 4787–895. Oxford: Wiley-Blackwell, 2010.

Scherer, James A. "Bartholomew Ziegenbalg." *Missiology* 27.4 (1999) 487–94.

Schmitz, Matthew. "Waiting for a Young Pope." *First Things* (March 2017) 71–72.

Schneewind, J. B. *The Invention of Autonomy.* New York: Cambridge University Press, 1998.

Sesboue, Bernard. "Tradition et traditions." *Nouvelle revue theologique* 112 (1990) 570–85.

Shils, Edward. *Tradition.* Chicago: University of Chicago Press, 1981.

Siddiqui, Ataullah. *Christian-Muslim Dialogue in the Twentieth Century.* New York: St. Martin's, 1997.

Skolnik, Fred, and Michael Berenbaum. *Encyclopaedia Judaica.* 22 vols. Detroit: Macmillan Reference USA, 2007.

Smart, James D. "The Treacherousness of Tradition." *Interpretation: A Journal of Bible and Theology* 30 (1976) 18–25.

Smolicz, J. J. "The Concept of Tradition: A Humanistic Interpretation." *The Australian and New Zealand Journal of Sociology* 10 (1974) 75–83.

Strawn, Brent A. *The Old Testament Is Dying: A Diagnosis and Recommended Treatment* Grand Rapids: Baker Academic, 2017.

Sullivan, Francis. *Magisterium: Teaching Authority in the Catholic Church.* New York: Paulist, 1983.

Taylor, Charles. *A Secular Age.* Cambridge: Belknap Press of Harvard University Press, 2007.

Terman, Rochelle. "Islamophobia, Feminism, and the Politics of Critique." *Theory, Culture & Society* 33 (2015) 77–102.

Tilley, Terrence W. "Culture Warriors." *Tablet*, November 22, 2012. 9, 11.

Tönnies, Ferdinand. *Community and Association (Gemeinschaft und Gesellschaft).* Translated by Charles P. Loomis. London: Routledge and Paul, 1974.

Troeltsch, Ernst. "Die Krisis des Historismus." *Die neue Rundschau* 33 (1922) 572–90.

United States Conference of Catholic Bishops (USCCB). "Doctrinal Responsibilities: Approaches to Promoting Cooperation and Resolving Misunderstandings between Bishops and Theologians." June 17, 1989. Online. http://www.usccb.org/about/doctrine/publications/index.cfm.

Valliere, Paul. "Tradition." In *Encyclopedia of Religion*, edited by Lindsay Jones, 9267–81. Detroit: Macmillan Reference USA, 2005.

Valparaiso University. "History." Online. https://www.valpo.edu/christ-college/about/history.

Vethanayagamony, Peter. "St. Vedanayagam Sastriar and the Literary Inculturation of the Gospel." *Lutheran Forum* 49.2 (2015) 36–40.

Vigen, James. "Missions, Revivals, and Diakonia in the Malagasy Lutheran Church." *Lutheran Forum* 48.4 (2014) 35–38.

Von Hügel, Friedrich. *Introduction and Biographies.* Vol. 1 of *The Mystical Element of Religion as Studied in Saint Catherine of Genoa and Her Friends.* 2nd ed. London: James Clarke, 1961.

BIBLIOGRAPHY

———. *Letters to a Niece*. Vancouver: Regent College, 2001.

Wilson, Sarah Hinlicky. *Woman, Women, and the Priesthood in the Trinitarian Theology of Elisabeth Behr-Sigel*. Edinburgh: T&T Clark, 2013.

Yerushalmi, Yosef Hayyim. *Zakhor: Jewish History and Jewish Memory*. Seattle: University of Washington Press, 1996.

Zaretzke, Kenneth. "The Idea of Tradition." *Intercollegiate Review* 17 (1982) 85–96.

Index